TORNADO

TORNADO

Robin Jones

WHARNCLIFFE
TRANSPORT

PREVIOUS PAGE: A1 Pacific No 60163 Tornado prepares to depart from Goathland with a Pickering train on the North Yorkshire Moors Railway on 7 May. DAVE RODGERS

First published in Great Britain in 2009 by
Mortons Media Group Ltd
Reprinted in this format in 2011 by
Wharncliffe Transport
an imprint of
Pen and Sword Books Limited,
47 Church Street, Barnsley,
South Yorkshire. S70 2AS

Copyright © Robin Jones, 2009, 2011

ISBN: 978 1 84468 120 4

The right of Robin Jones to be identified as author of this work has been asserted by him in accordance with the Copyright, Designs and Patents Act, 1988.

A CIP catalogue record of this book is available from the British Library.

Layout by Mac Style, Beverley, East Yorkshire
Printed in China through Printworks Int. Ltd.

Pen & Sword Books Ltd incorporates the imprints of
Pen & Sword Aviation, Pen & Sword Maritime,
Pen & Sword Military, Wharncliffe Local History, Pen & Sw
Pen & Sword Military Classics, Leo Cooper, Remember Wh
Seaforth Publishing and Frontline Publishing

For a complete list of Pen & Sword titles please contact:
PEN & SWORD BOOKS LIMITED
47 Church Street, Barnsley, South Yorkshire, S70 2AS, England.
E-mail: enquiries@pen-and-sword.co.uk
Website: www.pen-and-sword.co.uk

CONTENTS

With A1 Trust chairman Mark Allatt on the footplate, Tornado rounds the curve at Kinchley Lane with one of its first loaded test runs on the Great Central Railway on 24 August 2008. BRIAN SHARPE

Chapter 1

A LEGEND IS BORN…

You will never have read a railway book like this before. Indeed, it is far more than another book about trains – it is an account of a national achievement of heroic proportions; a dazzling achievement and one of which every last person in 21st-century Britain can be truly proud.

It is the story of how a small group of people who wanted to recreate one of the lost glories of the steam era came together in 1990 with no more than a shared dream – and 19 years later, turned it into reality. Without the benefit of an established railway workshop, or the workforce and facilities that were readily available to British Railways, they built a brand new main line express passenger locomotive from scratch.

Asking supporters to donate the price of a pint of beer a week to build the locomotive, A1 Peppercorn Pacific No 60163 *Tornado* has been built at a cost of £3 million, and tens of thousands of pounds of gruelling man-hours.

The first steam engine built for use on Britain's passenger network since Evening Star emerged from Swindon Works in a blaze of publicity in 1960, *Tornado* – named in honour of the RAF fighter pilots who served in the Gulf War – entered service on the main line on 31 January 2009.

At that time, Britain was reeling from the start of a deepening global recession, leaving ordinary people very little to cheer about. Except that is, an engineering feat of Herculean magnitude, one which gripped the imagination of the world's media and the public alike, from the Royal Family downwards.

Everywhere *Tornado* goes, crowds have packed station platforms and flocked to the lineside to grab a glimpse of it, resplendent in its apple green livery, jostling to capture images of it on mobile telephones. At every bridge, cutting or vantage point on every trip there are photographers who have driven many miles to capture this magnificent feat of engineering in action. Heritage railways which have hired *Tornado* for galas and special events have reported record attendances, despite the credit crunch.

Its performances on the national network have been stunning; bearing in mind the modifications that have had to be made to meet the requirements of the modern rail network, there are those who say that it is the most sophisticated steam

locomotive to ever run on Britain's railways. Apart from all that, the building of *Tornado* has filled a major gap in our nation's fleet of heritage steam locomotives. For back in 1966, nobody was able to save the last of the class of 49 London & North Eastern Railway-designed A1 Pacifics, which first appeared in 1948.

Railways have always proved an object of fascination; and even before the end of steam was announced, there were enthusiasts who were prepared to give their time free of charge to do their best to ensure that certain lines would not die, and classic locomotives would be saved from the scrapman.

This book tells how the railway preservation movement took off with the saving of the Talyllyn Railway in 1950, and set a ball rolling which nearly six decades later reached dizzy new heights with the launch of the project to build *Tornado*, the 50th A1. The full account of how the *Tornado* team came together to form The A1 Steam Locomotive Trust, the mammoth fundraising task and the building of the locomotive are outlined in detail.

The landmark day when the first fire was lit in the locomotive, its first movements in front of the world's press, its passenger-carrying debut on the Great Central Railway, its unveiling in its final livery at its base of the National Railway

Museum at York – where it will be on public display between its trips in the north of England – and its main line debut are fully covered.

Then there is the official naming ceremony carried out by TRH The Princes of Wales and The Duchess of Cornwall, *Tornado's* triumphant first entry and exit into and out of King's Cross, and the 'secret' filming assignment for BBC's *Top Gear* motoring programme, which saw it racing a classic 1940s car and motorcycle from London to Edinburgh.

This is the definitive account of how an impossible dream was made possible. One which evokes the very best of the British bulldog spirit – a classic tale of how the little man can succeed against overwhelming odds. A story which, in these times of failed bankers and politicians living luxury lifestyles through dubious expense claims, emerges like a shining beacon and a unique source of national pride to show the whole world what this country is still really all about. A tale that truly places the 'Great' back in Britain.

Thanks, that is, to the suporters of The A1 Steam Locomotive Trust, who have emerged in these despairing times as true national heroes, head and shoulders above the rest.

A SMART TURN OUT

CURTIS MOFFAT

"THE FLYING SCOTSMAN"

LEAVES KING'S CROSS LONDON
AND WAVERLEY STATION EDINBURGH
EVERY WEEKDAY AT 10 A.M.

LONDON & NORTH EASTERN RAILWAY

PUBLISHED BY THE LONDON & NORTH EASTERN RAILWAY   PRINTED IN GREAT BRITAIN   VINCENT BROOKS, DAY & SON, LTD., LITH., LONDON W.C.2

Chapter 2

THE GREAT PACIFIC HIGHWAY

W hen he performed the official naming ceremony of *Tornado*, HRH the Prince of Wales remarked to bystanders on the platform at York station that the first Peppercorn A1 4-6-2, or 'Pacific' as the wheel arrangement is universally known, was outshopped in 1948, the same year in which he was born.

However, the complete story of *Tornado* may be held to have begun more than a century before, with the building of the East Coast Main Line, the route for which

Great Northern Railway Stirling single 4-2-2 No 1, built in 1870 and representative of a type which ruled the roost on the East Coast Main Line in late Victorian times before the coming of the Pacifics, stands at the head of a rake of preserved teak coaches during the Doncaster 150 works open weekend in 2003. ROBIN JONES

Its boiler ticket having expired several years ago, streamlined recordholder A4 No 4468 Mallard is now one of the most popular exhibits at the National Railway Museum in York. ROBIN JONES

the A1s, like the other London & North Eastern Railway Pacifics before them, were designed.

Today the line is one of Britain's premier rail routes, running from London King's Cross to Edinburgh and on to Aberdeen. However, like so many other routes whose origins lie in the mid-19th century, it came together in stages, being built by three separate railway companies.

The North British Railway completed its line from Edinburgh to Berwick-on-

The village of Offord Cluny south of Huntingdon celebrates its proud East Coast Main Line heritage with this sign depicting Mallard's exploits. ROBIN JONES

The pioneer of the original Class A1 4-6-2s, No 4470 Great Northern, emerges from Wood Green tunnel on a down express, c1930. The first 11 Class A1s were built to the more generous Great Northern Railway loading gauge with a taller chimney, dome and cab. No 4470 was cut down to the composite LNER loading gauge in May 1933. **NATIONAL RAILWAY MUSEUM**

Tweed in 1846. It was followed by the Great Northern Railway from Shaftholme north of Doncaster to King's Cross, completed in 1850, and finally the North Eastern Railway from Berwick-on-Tweed to what became Shaftholme Junction, completed in 1871. To facilitate easy through running over the route, the companies jointly set up a pool of rolling stock in 1860 known as the East Coast Joint Stock.

The first through express service from King's Cross to Edinburgh began in 1864. The most important train, the 10am departure from London, became known as the 'Flying Scotsman'.

In 1923, the three became part of the LNER, which appointed Herbert Nigel Gresley as chief mechanical engineer – and who went on to design some of the world's most powerful express locomotives specifically for the route.

Mallard on Sunday 3 July 1938 at Barkston on the East Coast Main Line just prior to its record-breaking run when it reached 126mph between Grantham and Peterborough. NATIONAL RAILWAY MUSEUM

LEFT: Poster produced for the LNER to promote the 'Flying Scotsman' non-stop service between King's Cross, London, and Waverley, Edinburgh. The artwork is by Frank Newbould (1887-1951), who studied at Bradford College of Art and joined the War Office in 1942. He designed posters for the LNER, GWR, Orient Line and Belgian Railways. NATIONAL RAILWAY MUSEUM

Its LNER apple green livery having been applied at the 11th hour, the reborn No. 4472 Flying Scotsman – complete with double chimney – proudly stands at King's Cross on the morning of Sunday 4 July 1999 while passengers board the historic Inaugural Scotsman train to York to mark its comback. ROBIN JONES

Gresley, the most famous locomotive designer associated with the company, was born in 1876 and began his railway career as an apprentice at the London & North Western Railway's Crewe Works under FW Webb, during the legendary Races to the North. That was the period where the LNWR competed on the West Coast Main Line with the operators of the East Coast Main Line as to who could reach Scotland in the fastest time from London, and the locomotive development of the day was pushed to its limits as a result.

Gresley moved to the Lancashire & Yorkshire Railway in 1898 and worked under the engineer JAF Aspinall, becoming the foreman of the Blackpool running sheds. By 1904 he had become the company's assistant superintendent,

Gresley became the superintendent of the Great Northern Railway's carriage and wagon department in 1905 at the age of 29, beginning his close association with Doncaster.

In 1911, he became the chief mechanical engineer of the GNR, and his first locomotives showed signs of the innovation that would later become his trademark.

Two new streamlined Princess Coronation Pacifics take pride of place at Camden in 1938, as the LMS launched West Coast Main Line competition to rival the LNER and Nigel Gresley's A4 Pacifics. ROBIN JONES COLLECTION

A painting by M Secretan of LNER Gresley P2 three-cylinder 2-8-2 express locomotive No 2001 Cock o' the North, designed specifically to overcome the difficulties posed by the severe gradients and tight curves of the line between Edinburgh and Aberdeen. It was the first eight-coupled locomotive to be built in Britain for express passenger service. The locomotive was completed in 1934, but although its performance was in many ways excellent, it did not deal effectively with the problems of sharp curves on the route for which it had been designed. It was later and very controversially rebuilt by Edward Thompson. NATIONAL RAILWAY MUSEUM

The front of King's Cross station as seen in the 1920s. LONDON TRANSPORT MUSEUM ©TRANSPORT FOR LONDON

His large-boilered three-cylinder express goods K3 2-6-0 appeared in 1920, while, most importantly to our purposes here, his first three-cylinder Pacific, No 1470 *Great Northern*, a member on an earlier class numbered A1 (later A3), appeared in April 1922.

Gresley chose a Big Engine policy for the LNER, largely because of its premier route. In September 1922, No 1471 pulled a 600-ton test train, underlining the abilities of the glamorous new class.

The A1s certainly showed their ability to haul heavy loads on the East Coast Main Line, but proved inefficient with coal and water, as highlighted during the 1925 Great Western Exchange Trials, when they were beaten in this aspect by the older Great Western Railway Castle 4-6-0s. Adjustments to valve settings led to a major improvement in coal consumption and all A1s were accordingly modified by 1931.

Gresley streamlined A4 No 4467 Wild Swan leaves King's Cross with the 'Northern Belle' in 1939. NATIONAL RAILWAY MUSEUM

Another improvement came in 1926 when all of the piston valve rings on the A1s were replaced in order to reduce frictional heating losses.

Between 1927 and 1947, all of the original A1s were rebuilt as A3s, with the exception of *Great Northern*, which was rebuilt by Gresley's successor Edward Thompson in 1945 as Class A1/1. The rebuild involved increasing the number of flues in the Robinson superheater and raising the boiler pressure from 180psi to 220psi with the first five new boilers being ordered in 1927.

From then on, all new Pacifics were built to the A3 specification rather than the A1. In 1937, the Kylchap double blastpipe arrangement was fitted to No 2751 *Humorist*, requiring the use of smoke deflectors. The A1s and A3s were so successful that all 79 were inherited by British Railways at nationalisation in 1948. The development of the class continued, with A4 boilers being fitted to A3s from 1954, and Kylchap blastpipes and chimneys between 1958 and 1959 to all the remaining A3s, requiring the use of German-style smoke deflectors, although not all A3s recieved the deflectors.

Gresley died suddenly in 1941. Thompson, who had been promoted to workshop manager of Stratford Works in London in 1930, disagreed with Gresley on many aspects of locomotive development.

As chief mechanical engineer, Thompson began a much-needed programme of standardisation, while illustrating some contempt for his predecessor by rebuilding several of his classic designs, like the V2 express goods 2-6-2s, P2 Mikado 2-8-2s and the original A1 the prototype *Great Northern*. There were many who were angered by his choice of *Great Northern* to be rebuilt, and implored in vain for him to choose another locomotive.

However, once the controversial rebuilding had been carried out, the locomotive was arguably a better performer than other Gresley Pacifics and over the years gave excellent service at many sheds, despite being a one-off that had comparatively little relation to the Peppercorn class that was also to be classified A1.

Thompson retired in 1946, his brief and often vilified reign having been dogged by wartime conditions, which severely restricted his scope for locomotive development.

His first Pacific venture was the rebuilding of Gresley's six P2s class 2-8-2s, for the sake of standardisation, despite the fact that they were regarded very much as status symbols. The rebuilds were classified as A2/2s and were the first of the Thompson rebuilds to be withdrawn.

The next batch of Thompson Pacifics were based around spare Gresley V2 boilers and components from locomotives already ordered, and were classified A2/1s.

The final series of Thompson A2s were all-new engines but similar in appearance to the rebuilt locomotives and were classified by BR as A2/3s.

However, by far the most famous of all LNER Pacifics – as a class – were the streamlined A4s, their air-smoothed casing embodying 1930s luxury and the contemporary fascination with steam speed.

At the time, competition from road transport was beginning to bite, and the railway companies realised that travel between cities had to be both faster and more appealing.

High-speed diesel trains generated headlines across the world. May 1933 saw the Deutsche Bundesbhan diesel-electric Fliegende Hamburger make its debut, covering long distances at 85mph, and the following year, the US Burlington Zephyr hit 112.5mph. Both, however, were only two and three-car units.

The LNER agreed to a series of trials, during which time No 4472 *Flying Scotsman* became the first steam locomotive to officially break the 100mph barrier on 30 November 1934, and sister No 2750 *Papyrus* attained average speeds almost as fast as the Fliegende Hamburger but with a larger coach capacity, setting a speed record of 108mph in the process.

Because of the success of these trials, Gresley's plans for a 'Silver Jubilee' train with streamlined locomotives and matching coaches were given the green light.

With these trials under his belt, the LNER Board gave Gresley the go-ahead to create the 'Silver Jubilee' streamlined trains.

The distinctive wedge-shaped casings on the A4s drew from the design of a Bugatti railcar, which Gresley had seen in France, and modified with the help of the wind tunnel facilities at the National Physical Laboratory at Teddington.

The streamlined A4s were a gift from heaven for the LNER publicity department.

But behind the casings, there were several major modifications from the A1s/A3s. The boiler pressure was increased from 220psi to 250psi, while the cylinders were decreased slightly in size so that the valve diameters could be increased to 9in, so as to produce free steaming within the restrictions of the three-cylinder design.

All of the steam passages were streamlined, and as with the A3, Walschaerts gear was used on the outside cylinders, and Gresley's conjugated gear for the inside cylinder. Further refinements including the Kylchap double-blastpipe exhaust were added at a later date.

A demonstration run from King's Cross to Grantham on 27 September 1935 reached 112.5mph. No 2509 *Silver Link* launched the first service on 1 October that year.

The service slashed the travel time between King's Cross and Newcastle down to four hours for the first time. Accordingly, the service was extended to Edinburgh, and to Leeds & Bradford in 1937. A total of 35 A4s were built to service what was seen as Britain's first inter-city network of fast train services.

The LNER's chief rival, the London, Midland & Scottish Railway, was not taking it lying down. Its Chief Mechanical Engineer came up with a streamlined locomotive set to rival the 'Silver Jubilee' and Gresley's A4s.

On 28 June 1937, the LMS streamlined 'Coronation Scot' set a new record of 114mph.

Because braking distances were getting longer with increased speeds, improved braking was essential, and Gresley chose a system developed by Westinghouse that was already used by the LMS, with trials beginning in 1938.

On 3 July 1938, a test train was run along the East Coast from King's Cross to Barkston Junction and back behind A4 No 4468 *Mallard*.

At Grantham, on the way back, Gresley told those on board that the train was going to go for the steam speed record, and if anybody wished, they could alight at that point. Everyone stayed in their seats.

On Stoke Bank, 120mph was achieved between mileposts 92.75 and 89.75, and for 306 yards, 125mph was touched. A peak of 126mph was marked on the dynamometer rolls, beating the 124.5mph set by Deutsche Bundesbahn and setting a record for steam that has never been broken.

In late June 1962, Copley Hill-based A1 No 60120 Kittiwake drifts into Grantham with a northbound train that is signalled to stop. CECIL VOGEL/A1SLT

Chapter 3

PEPPERCORN'S MAGNIFICENT MACHINES

Thompson was succeeded by Arthur H Peppercorn, then aged 57. Born in Leominster, Herefordshire, on 29 January 1889, Peppercorn commenced his career as a Great Northern Railway apprentice in 1905, serving with the Royal Engineers in World War One.

The first Peppercorn A1 Pacific, No 60114 later to be named WP Allen. In 1948 and 1949, British Railways built, at its Doncaster and Darlington Works, 49 Peppercorn A1s. The earlier Gresley Pacifics were three-cylinder machines which drove all cylinders on to the middle axle; Peppercorn used divided drive, with the middle cylinder connected to the leading axle. Gresley had used conjugated valve gear, while Peppercorn used three sets of Walschaerts. And Peppercorn used a markedly larger grate, of 50 sq ft – the same as that used by Gresley on his magnificent P2s. COLOUR-RAIL

The man and machine: Arthur H Peppercorn leans out of the cab of his LNER A2 Pacific No 525 after it was officially named in his honour at Marylebone station on 18 December 1947. NATIONAL RAILWAY MUSEUM

Many saw his appointment as reverting to the good old days of Gresley, and he pleased many at Doncaster Works by reappointing some of Gresley's former assistants.

He was in charge for just 18 months before nationalisation, and was left to complete many of Thompson's locomotives.

When Peppercorn took over, he halted production on a batch of 30 Thompson-designed mixed-traffic Pacifics after only 15 had been built. The remaining 15 were modified to Peppercorn's own design.

In broad terms, he combined the best aspects of Gresley and Thompson designs.

As David Elliott, director of engineering at The A1 Steam Locomotive Trust, which built *Tornado*, explained: "The research we did in the National Railway Museum at York saw us look at lots of drawings of earlier engines as well as our own.

"We saw just how much detailed design development work went on between the Gresley A1 in 1922 and the A4s in 1935.

"Although Thompson's Pacifics in the 40s were not generally regarded as highly successful engines, he incorporated a number of things which appeared in the Peppercorn A1s, such as rocking gates, hopper ashpans and very good quality steam circuits from the superheater header through the cylinders and up the

LNER A2 Pacific No 525 Arthur H Peppercorn. NATIONAL RAILWAY MUSEUM

chimney. In some respects these were better than in the Gresley period and were continued in the Peppercorn development of the Pacifics.

"Peppercorn himself really took the Thompson locomotives forward and eradicated some of the Thompson designs which were actually worse than what Gresley had done before, particularly this unfortunate adherence to coupling rods the same length on all cylinders, which caused the outside cylinders to be placed behind the bogie. (This was the wartime standardisation priority principle of having all the connecting rods the same length).

"The problem is that the other major Thompson change from Gresley's days was a full set of Walschaerts valve gear in between the frames and dividing the drive. It left no room for adequate bracing between the frames.

"With the cylinders so far back, they flexed a lot, which caused trouble with frame fractures and constant problems with leaking steam pipes.

"Peppercorn rightly put the A2 cylinders back in the conventional Gresley position on the outside, which moved them forward nearer to the middle cylinder, considerably strengthening the frame structure in the process, and so did away with all the problems with leaky steam pipes. It made the engines about 2ft shorter, but they looked very much more pleasant."

A1 No 60158 Aberdonian departs from King's Cross with A4 No 60031 Golden Plover, carrying the headboard of the London to Edinburgh 'The Elizabethan' service, alongside. ERIC TREACY/NRM

A1 No 60131 Osprey at Wakefield Westgate station. The photographer – the late Bishop Eric Treacy. Treacy (1907–1978) was often allowed special access to areas denied to many railway photographers. He also befriended many of the footplate crews, occasionally persuading them to create special smoke effects for the camera. ERIC TREACY/NRM

Also, somewhat strangely, Peppercorn's A2s went back to having a single chimney in a period in which double chimneys were becoming widely adopted.

However, the final few Peppercorn A2s reverted to a double chimney – a standard feature on his A1 Pacifics.

The A2s proved to be good, solid locomotives, if not spectacular performers. After several years of service exclusively on the East Coast Main Line, many were despatched to Scotland working both from Edinburgh and later from Glasgow's Polmadie and Corkerhill sheds. Much of their final passenger work was between Dundee or Aberdeen and Glasgow.

Peppercorn also built a mixed traffic 2-6-0, the K1, based on Thompson's two-cylinder rebuild of Gresley's K4 three-cylinder 2-6-0.

Peppercorn's last and only other engines were his A1s.

Despite its dire post-war economic situation, and despite already having more Pacifics than any of the other railways, the LNER found itself (after the Southern Railway had unveiled its Bulleid 4-6-2s) as the only one of the 'Big Four' companies to be still designing and building new Pacifics in the late 40s.

A1 60156 Great Central by the coaling tower at 'Top Shed', 34A Kings Cross, in April 1957. PETER TOWNEND/A1SLT

A1 No 60157 Great Eastern exiting Gasworks Tunnel at Belle Isle just outside King's Cross with the 'Tees Tyne Pullman' of 30 May 1957. PETER TOWNEND/A1SLT

The A1 design recalled the 6ft 8in big-wheeled express locomotive capable of long runs at high speeds.

Many of Thompson's ideas, like the divided drive, separate valve gears for each cylinder and the large free-steaming boiler with a very big firebox, formed part of the Peppercorn A1 blueprint.

The production A1 Pacifics were built under Peppercorn's jurisdiction, but did not appear until BR days – hence their appearance in LNER apple green with BRITISH RAILWAYS in big lettering along the tender, as carried by *Tornado* today.

The first, No 60114, emerged from Doncaster Works on 6 August 1948, three weeks before the last A2.

A total of 49 were built inside just 16 months, Nos 60114-60129 and 60153-60162 at Doncaster and the rest at Darlington.

They were allocated to sheds all across former LNER territory – King's Cross, Doncaster, Gateshead, Grantham, York, Copley Hill, Haymarket and Heaton.

Capable of extremely hard work, the Peppercorn A1s had a deserved reputation for free steaming and very sound performances on any task. Not only that, but they also managed very high mileages between overhauls.

No 60157 Great Eastern leaving King's Cross goods yard with the 3.15pm 266 Down goods, in the hands of driver Duckmanton on 11 June 1957. PETER TOWNEND/A1SLT

On the East Coast Main Line, Peppercorn A1s were the only locomotives to increase steam pressure while working hard and with both injectors in use to fill the boiler with water.

Firemen had to accommodate the needs of the larger grate to maintain economy in the use of coal and water.

The power available from the A1 boiler allowed crews to work them hard to recover time after delays. Nevertheless, there are few records of them exceeding 100mph compared to the A4s, in whose pre-war shadow the class unfortunately and often unjustly had to live, although there is at least one report of 108mph being reached.

Over the years, claims have been made that the A1s were rough riders. While that may have been true in the latter days of steam when maintenance was too often neglected in favour of diesels, most crews found the ride to be comfortable and steady, albeit not as smooth as that offered by an A4. Indeed, many drivers preferred the Peppercorn A1s to any other LNER class.

Sadly, none of the A1s were ever fitted with a corridor tender and so never had the chance to fulfil glamour workings on big-name trains like 'The Elizabethan'.

The Thompson and Peppercorn engines had steam brakes whereas the Gresley locomotives, which had corridor tenders, were fitted with vacuum brakes, and so the tenders between the different types were not transferable. The original proposal for the Peppercorn A1s had them fitted with corridor tenders, but they did not materialise.

A1 Great Eastern awaits duty at King's Cross shed on 2 March 1959. PETER TOWNEND/A1SLT

Nos 60140 Balmoral and 60146 Peregrine in York roundhouse in 1964. This building is now the National Railway Museum, occasional home of the 50th Peppercorn A1, Tornado. JOHN ARNOTT-BROWN/A1SLT

Three A1s together: No 60117 Bois Roussel at King's Cross 'Top Shed' with A4 No 60033 Seagull and A3 No 60108 Gay Crusader in August 1959. PETER TOWNEND/A1SLT

A1 No 60118 Archibald Sturrock, in poor condition near the end of its life, prepares to head south from Darlington Bank Top station in 1964. JOHN ARNOTT-BROWN/A1SLT

Two of the many A1s allocated to Gateshead, Nos 60154 and 60155, were fitted with roller bearings, and may well have accordingly turned in the finest performances of any members of the class.

The last chief mechanical engineer of the LNER, Peppercorn retired in 1949 when his position was abolished. He died on 3 March 1951, and is survived by his widow, Mrs Dorothy Mather – who is now president of The A1 Steam Locomotive Trust, which has built the 50th Peppercorn A1 Pacific, No 60163 *Tornado*.

The Peppercorn Pacifics had a short career with an average life span of just 15 years – and less than a decade of top-link working – because of the onset of modernisation.

Their first 10 years saw them doing most of their work on the East Coast Main Line apart from three sent to Polmadie shed in the mid-50s for working some of the West Coast Main Line expresses from Glasgow as far as Carlisle.

As the East Coast Main Line became dieselised, with the Class 55 Deltics taking over top-link duties from 1961 onwards, more and more A1s and A2s were moved northwards and relegated to secondary duties.

Towards the end of steam, they worked over Scottish lines like the Waverley route and to Aberdeen. They could also be glimpsed on the Settle to Carlisle and

A1 PACIFICS

A1/1 4470 60113 Great Northern	A1 60139 Sea Eagle
A1 60114 WP Allen	A1 60140 Balmoral
A1 60115 Meg Merrillies	A1 60141 Abbottsford
A1 60116 Hal o' the Wynd	A1 60142 Edward Fletcher
A1 60117 Bois Roussel	A1 60143 Sir Walter Scott
A1 60118 Archibald Sturrock	A1 60144 King's Courier
A1 60119 Patrick Stirling	A1 60145 Saint Mungo
A1 60120 Kittiwake	A1 60146 Peregrine
A1 60121 Silurian	A1 60147 North Eastern
A1 60122 Curlew	A1 60148 Aboyeur
A1 60123 HA Ivatt	A1 60149 Amadis
A1 60124 Kenilworth	A1 60150 Willbrook
A1 60125 Scottish Union	A1 60151 Midlothian
A1 60126 Sir Vincent Raven	A1 60152 Holyrood
A1 60127 Wilson Worsdell	A1 60153 Flamboyant
A1 60128 Bongrace	A1 60154 Bon Accord
A1 60129 Guy Mannering	A1 60155 Borderer
A1 60130 Kestrel	A1 60156 Great Central
A1 60131 Osprey	A1 60157 Great Eastern
A1 60132 Marmion	A1 60158 Aberdonian
A1 60133 Pommern	A1 60159 Bonnie Dundee
A1 60134 Foxhunter	A1 60160 Auld Reekie
A1 60135 Madge Wildfire	A1 60161 North British
A1 60136 Alcazar	A1 60162 Saint Johnstoun
A1 60137 Redgauntlet	A1 60163 Tornado
A1 60138 Boswell	

The last A1, No 60145 Saint Mungo, waits to depart from York station with the 6.30pm special to Newcastle on 31 December 1965. MAURICE BURNS

The sole surviving A2 Pacific: No 60532 Blue Peter seen climbing near Beck Hole with a Grosmont to Pickering service on the North Yorkshire Moors Railway on its return to steam on 26 December 1991. BRIAN SHARPE

No 60148 Aboyeur hands the southbound 'The Northumbrian' to No 60158 Aberdonian at Grantham in May 1953. PETER TOWNEND/A1SLT

No 60157 Great Eastern being cut up at Draper's Yard in Hull in March 1965. REV J DAVID BENSON/A1SLT

Glasgow & South Western lines from 1964, allocated to Neville Hill and working summer relief trains. They often turned in sterling performances when rescuing failed diesels.

The first A1 to be withdrawn was No 60123 *H. A. Ivatt*, following an accident near Offord in September 1962. The last Al to receive a general overhaul was No 60124 *Kenilworth* at Darlington North Road Works.

Withdrawals, however, gathered pace in 1964. At the start of 1965 there were 25 A1s still in service, but *Sir Vincent Raven*, *Balmoral*, *Bongrace* and *Great Eastern* were withdrawn in January.

Great Central was withdrawn in May, and the following month, *Aboyeur*, *Bois Roussel*, *Edward Fletcher*, *Holyrood*, *Hal'o the Wynd*, *Marmion*, *Pommern* and *Wilson Worsdell* steamed their last.

Archibald Sturrock, *Bon Accord*, *Boswell*, *Foxhunter*, *Guy Mannering*, *Kestrel*, *Osprey* and *Silurian* were withdrawn in October, with *Midlothian* following in November. That left only *Kenilworth* and *Saint Mungo*.

What had been an everyday sight on the North Eastern Region all but disappeared overnight.

The final advertised passenger run of an A1 was marketed by British Railways as a special to mark 'the end of express steam haulage on the North Eastern Region'.

The eight-coach train was to be run on New Year's Eve 1965, departing from Platform 14 in darkness at 6.30pm for Newcastle, and returning the same evening.

A wheel had turned full circle, as it was 140 years earlier that the Stockton & Darlington Railway had run the first passenger trains behind steam in the North East, or anywhere in the world for that matter.

Saint Mungo, the last working A1 hauled the train, and was duly turned out in immaculate condition, but without its nameplates.

Huge crowds forsook their seasonal festivities to turn out for the occasion. Union flags had been attached to the express code headlamps, and between the lamps. It was a moving occasion, almost unreal.

The departure was delayed by 20 minutes due to enthusiasts' specials from Bristol and the Midlands running late. With driver Harry Vince and fireman Ron Fenwick on the footplate, it finally left at 6.48pm.

As the A1 passed York shed, it gave a long whistle to the waving shed staff. A Thompson B1 which had been backing on the shed and a K1 on a freight working both whistled replies. The special approached the packed platforms at Thirsk at 80mph and hit 85mph shortly after Ferryhill.

Another massive crowd was at Newcastle along with waiting pressmen to greet the special as it pulled into Platform 10 at 8.25pm, before the crew was mobbed by enthusiasts wanting their autographs.

The return trip saw the A1 reach 90mph through Ferryhill. For the original 49 members of the class, it was a swansong.

The mighty English Electric Class 55 Deltics replaced the Pacifics on the East Coast Main Line. Preserved D9009 Alycidon is displayed at the National Railway Museum in 2008. ROBIN JONES

"THIS STEEL MAST WAS THE FIRST OF 33,000 TO BE ERECTED AS PART OF THE SCHEME TO ELECTRIFY THE EAST COAST MAIN LINE. IT WAS PLACED IN POSITION HERE ON THURSDAY, 7TH FEBRUARY, 1985, BY COUNCILLOR RAYMOND PALMER, J.P. MAYOR OF PETERBOROUGH, MR FRANK PATERSON, GENERAL MANAGER, BRITISH RAIL EASTERN REGION, AND MR DON HOLLAND, C.B.E CHAIRMAN OF BALFOUR BEATTY LTD."

Time marches on: the Deltics having been withdrawn four years earlier, this plaque at Peterborough station marks the erection in 1985 of the first mast for the East Coast Main Line electrification scheme. ROBIN JONES

David Elliott said: "I was recently told by Geoff Bird, shedmaster at York at the time, that *Saint Mungo* reached 102mph between Darlington and York on that trip – but it rattled and banged a bit."

Scrapping usually followed within weeks of withdrawal. *Kenilworth* was withdrawn at the end of March the following year, was sold on 5 June and scrapped shortly afterwards.

Saint Mungo ended its days in BR service when it was officially condemned on 19 June 1966 and was sold to scrap dealer AE Draper of Hull that August.

The original class therefore became extinct.

With the then-embryonic heritage railway movement gaining ground, two years later Draper decided to preserve a steam locomotive, but chose a LMS 'Black Five' 4-6-0, No 45305, which was subsequently named *Alderman A.E. Draper* and which is now in service on the Great Central Railway at Loughborough. Several 'Black Fives' were saved by preservationists, but sadly no A1.

However, an A2 did manage to survive, in the form of No 60532 *Blue Peter*. A Mr C Roads of Cambridge formed a preservation society and because someone was trying to save it, British Railway decided to give it a stay of execution.

Eventually, the Association of Railway Preservation Societies, the forerunner of today's Heritage Railway Association, took up its cause, and its efforts led to two enthusiasts, the late Geoff Drury and Brian Hollingsworth jointly buying it. Few would have believed it back in the mid-60s, but it would not be the last time that a Peppercorn A1 Pacific would grace the East Coast Main Line.

Following the appearance of the distinctive blue-liveried prototype English Electric Deltic, a fleet of 22 production models was built to replace steam on the East Coast Main Line express traffic. Powered by engines originally developed for fast torpedo boats, at 3300hp they are still the most powerful diesel locomotive to have entered service in Britain.

Following their introduction, the first sections of the East Coast Main Line were upgraded to officially allow 100 miles per hour running. The first length to be so approved was the 17 miles between Peterborough and Grantham on 15 June 1965.

In turn, the Deltics were superseded by the faster High Speed Train between 1976 and 1981.

The Government financed the electrification of the East Coast Main Line beginning in 1985, with the first section between King's Cross and Leeds undergoing trials in 1988. Full electrification was completed in late 1990, when InterCity 225 units were introduced.

Chapter 4

THE END OF
BRITISH STEAM

Britain was somewhat late in eradicating steam from its railway network and replacing it with diesel and electric traction. Such modernisation had begun in the USA in the 30s, but the newly nationalised British network began life still very much in the period of wartime austerity and ration books, and had insufficient finance to follow suit.

Nonetheless, in 1948, British Railways appointed Robert Riddles as its Chief Mechanical Engineer. Vice-president of the London Midland & Scottish Railway, he had excelled during the war with his designs for War Department Austerity 2-8-0s and 2-10-0s.

He was asked to produce a new modern fleet of steam locomotives to serve the national network, drawing on the best practices of the 'Big Four' companies in their design. In the event, the 12 Standard classes, which ranged from tank engines to express passenger locomotives, drew heavily on previous LMS designs.

The first, Britannia Pacific No 70000 *Britannia*, appeared in 1951, the same year as the Festival of Britain. It was followed by a further 998 Standards, with experts considering his 9F heavy freight 2-10-0s to be the best of all.

The final purpose-built express passenger steam locomotive to be built by BR turned out to be a one-off – Class 8P Pacific No 71000 *Duke of Gloucester*, which appeared from Crewe Works in 1954. It was also the last new express passenger steam locomotive to be built for the British main line... until *Tornado*.

It was ordered by BR as a direct replacement for LMS Princess Royal Pacific No 46202 *Princess Anne*, which was destroyed in the Harrow train crash of 8 October 1952 in which 112 people lost their lives. While the Duke shared many features common to the Britannias and his other Standard designs, Riddles chose to equip the locomotive with Caprotti valve gear.

Allocated to Crewe North, and set to work the 'Mid Day Scot' over Shap and Beattock, it had a mixed reaction among West Coast Main Line crews, many preferring the LMS Pacifics. Still very much an experimental locomotive, it encountered problems with steam production, and clearly needed adjustments to vastly improve its performance. They were never to be made, at least not by BR. No further members of the class were built, for in December 1954 came the BR Modernisation Plan, calling for the rapid replacement of steam locomotives with diesel and electric alternatives.

The last express passenger locomotive built by British Railways was Class 8P Pacific No 71000 Duke of Gloucester, seen in action at Goathland on the North Yorkshire Moors Railway on 30 September 2008. BRIAN SHARPE

Faced with increasing competition from road transport and soaring car ownership, the report aimed to bring the UK rail network into the 20th century, by increasing speed, reliability, safety and line capacity. A government White Paper of 1956 claimed that modernisation would help wipe out BR's financial deficit by 1962.

That did not happen, and many of the diesel types which were hurriedly produced to replace perfectly good steam locomotives proved less than

In 2008, the National Railway Museum held a special '1968 And All That' event to mark the 40th anniversary of the end of British Railways main line steam. Lined up are, left to right, GWR 4-6-0 No 5029 Nunney Castle, BR Britannia 4-6-2 No 70013 Oliver Cromwell (the last main line steam engine overhauled by BR and hauling the final passenger train) and Evening Star. ROBIN JONES

Much was made by British Railways of the official naming of its final steam locomotive, 9F 2-10-0 No 92220 Evening Star, at Swindon on 18 March 1960. It would be Britain's last new main line steam locomotive until Tornado undertook its test trips in late 2008. PAUL CHANCELLOR COLLECTION

satisfactory, and several did not outlive steam. However, BR continued to turn out steam locomotives which had been ordered, the last being 9F No 92220 *Evening Star*.

The 251st in the class, and officially named at its Swindon Works birthplace on 18 March 1960, *Evening Star* was the last main line steam locomotive built for BR. It would also be the last new steam locomotive to appear on the national network for nearly half a century, again, until the appearance of *Tornado*.

Evening Star – now preserved and on static display inside the STEAM Museum at Swindon because of its immense historical importance – was not, however, the last new steam locomotive built in Britain at the end of the 'steam age'.

It was in 1963 that the last order for two steam locomotives for British use was received by a UK manufacturer. Standard gauge Hunslet Austerity 0-6-0STs Nos 3889 and 3890 were finished on 18 March and 23 March respectively.

Although they were built purely for industrial use, for the National Coal Board, arguably they were main line types as they were all but identical to the Hunslet Austerity 0-6-0STs, a hugely successful World War Two design, some of which taken into main line service as the LNER's J94 class.

Both engines were sold for £15,000 each. No 3889 was sent to Manvers Coal Preparation Plant and No 3890 to Cadeby Main Colliery, Conisborough, where it became No 66 in the South Yorkshire NCB fleet.

The pair were originally fitted with mechanical stokers to assist in the one-man operation, and a gas producer to reduce smoke emission, in a last-ditch bid to extend the life of the steam locomotive concept.

However, the gas producer system and mechanical stoker on No 3890 fell into disuse, and conventional methods of firing were adopted, with an ordinary grate being fitted. As a result, when Conisborough was designated a smokeless zone in 1970, the locomotive, the 484th Austerity to be built, had to be replaced by a second-hand BR diesel shunter.

No 3890, therefore the last standard gauge steam engine built in Britain, is now stored at the Buckinghamshire Railway Centre, where it needs a heavy overhaul, while No 3889 has spent recent years at the Rutland Railway Museum, repainted into the bright yellow livery it carried in NCB service.

The pair emerged from Hunslet's Leeds works a year after it outshopped another 'brand new' Austerity, No 3851, which in reality was assembled from parts left over from the last batch of 0-6-0STs built in the early 50s. It went to Leicestershire's Nailstone Colliery. Hunslet also bought 14 second-hand Austerities from the Army and extensively rebuilt them as all-but-new locomotives between 1961 and 1970, managing to sell all but three.

In 1962, Hunslet carried out the almost-complete rebuilding of Snowdon Mountain Railway's Swiss SLM, 1896-built 0-4-2T No 4 *Snowdon*, which had lain derelict at Llanberis for many years. Only the frame plates and one cylinder from the original locomotive saw service again, and so it may well be considered to be a

The world's other last steam locomotive

- Famed British builder Andrew Barclay's last steam locomotive was works No 2377, an 0-6-2 supplied to Indonesia in September 1962, the order having been transferred from WG Bagnall & Co which had by then ceased building after supplying works No 3126, a 2-8-2 narrow gauge tender engine, to the Mysore Iron & Steel Works in India.

- Hudswell Clarke's last steam locomotive appeared in 1961, 0-4-0ST No 1893 for the National Coal Board.

- Peckett's last steam engine was works No 2165 of 1958, a 3ft gauge 0-6-0T for the Sena Sugar Estates in Mozambique.

- Robert Stephenson & Hawthorns produced its last conventional steam locomotive in 1958, 0-6-0ST No 8051 for Stewarts & Lloyd's Hungarford Quarry.

- The last Robert Stephenson & Hawthorns steam engine was six-coupled fireless locomotive, No 8082, delivered to the NCB's Glasshaughton coking plant in January 1959.

- Vulcan Foundry turned out its 6204th and final steam engine on 13 June 1956, completing an order for 46 2-8-4s for the East African Railways.

- The Sentinel works of Shrewsbury produced its last steam engines in 1957.

- The Yorkshire Engine Company's last steam engines were pannier tanks ordered by the BR Western Region in 1949, the last, No 3409 (works No 2584), being delivered in 1956.

- The final steam engines built by the North British Locomotive Company were four 2-8-2s for Nyasaland, Nos 27779-27782, the last being steamed in early February 1958.

- The USSR ceased passenger steam locomotive building in 1956, when the final L class 2-10-0s, LV 2-10-2s and P36 4-8-4s were turned out.

- When Norfolk & Western Railroad S1a class 0-8-0 shunter No 244 emerged from Roanoke works in December 1953, it was the final steam locomotive built for service in North America.

- The last steam engines built by the US manufacturer Baldwin were 50 WG class 2-8-2s for the Indian 5ft 6ins broad gauge in 1955. The final Baldwin built for US use was a 2-8-0 supplied to the US Army Transportation School at Fort Eustis in Virginia in 1952.

- In Australia, the final steam locomotive to be built was B18 class 4-6-2 No 1089 in 1958, turned out by Walkers of Maryland for the 3ft 6ins gauge Queensland Government Railways.

- The last steam locomotive to debut on the French main line in SNCF service was Corpet, Louvet et Compagnie 2-10-2T 151 TQ22 No 1920 on 30September 1952. Two SACM 0-6-0Ts supplied to the Cévennes mines system in 1953 were believed to be the last steam engines built in France for industrial use.

- Indian Railways' Chittaranjan Works ceased building steam engines in 1972, when a YG class metre gauge locomotive was the last. However, Indian Railways' Golden Rock Works built two new 0-4-0STs for the Darjeeling Himalayan Railway in 2003, numbered 1001/1002. However, are they 'real' steam engines like Trangkil No 4, or 'heritage', as new steam traction rather than diesel was selected because of its tourist appeal?

- Poland's Fablok locomotive plant in Chrzanów built its last steam engine for state railway company PKP, TKt48-191, in 1957, but turned out its last industrial freight engine, World War Two German-design 0-4-0 T2D-6293, in 1963.

- West Germany's last main line steam locomotive to enter service was Class 23 No 23-105 in 1959.

- The last new steam engine built in the former Czechoslovakia was 4-8-4T No 464.202, built by Skoda in 1955.

- China's Tangshan Works outshopped standard gauge SY class 2-8-2 No 1772 in October 1999, and some regard it as the last steam locomotive to be built in the country. It is based at Tiefa and runs on a line operated by the Daqin Coal Company. Is it therefore the last 'real' main line locomotive, tourist and heritage projects apart, to be built in the world?

Britain's last 'real' steam locomotive, Hunslet 0-4-2ST No 3902 of 1971 Trangkil No 4, seen in action on the Statfold Barn Railway after being reimported from Java. ROBIN JONES

Three years after Evening Star appeared, Hunslet of Leeds built Britain's last all-new standard gauge steam locomotive, Austerity 0-6-0 saddle tank No 3890, seen here at Buckinghamshire Railway Centre, its importance so often overlooked. BOB FRISE/BRC

Britain's penultimate standard gauge locomotive, Austerity 0-6-0ST No 3889 of 1963, at the Rutland Railway Museum. ROBIN JONES

Hunslet new build. Also in 1962, Hunslet supplied the last two of a batch of 0-6-2Ts for the 2ft 6ins gauge Nepal Jaynagar-Janakpur Railway.

In 1967, Hunslet helped build a new batch of 2ft gauge NGG16 articulated Beyer Garatts for South African Railways, and supplied eight boilers to Hunslet Taylor Consolidated in Johannesburg.

The first locomotive exported by Hunslet had gone to Java in 1866, two years after the firm was founded. Ironically, it was the last 'steam era' (as opposed to preservation or heritage era) engine to be built in Britain, also by Hunslet, that went to the same island nation.

Ordered in 1970 by Robert Hudson (Raletrux) Ltd for the Trangkil sugar factory system near Surabayas, the design of No 3902 – which became *Trangkil No 4* – dated back to 1909, and was hardly cutting-edge technology. Indeed, it was mechanically the same as the firm's Tamar class built for the Cameroons in 1952.

As it had been some years since Hunslet had built a new narrow gauge steam engine, it appeared that staff hunted throughout the Leeds factory and found enough spare parts to fulfil the order.

The rights to the Hunslet name were later bought by businessman and multi-millionaire enthusiast Graham Lee, who re-established a locomotive workshop using the historic firm's name at his private Statfold Barn Railway in Tamworth, Staffordshire.

Not only that, but he repatriated no less than No 3902 from Java and had it rebuilt at Statfold Barn. It reappeared in as-built condition hauling passenger trains there during an invited guests-only open day in June 2005.

Main line steam ended on British Railways on 11 August 1968, with the running of the '15 Guinea Special' from Liverpool Lime Street. Among the locomotives which hauled the train was Britannia Pacific No 70013 *Oliver Cromwell,* the last steam engine overhauled by BR.

After that date, steam haulage was replaced by modern traction on all but BR's sole surviving narrow gauge line, the Vale of Rheidol Railway. Inherited from the GWR in 1948, its tourist appeal saw it survive threats of closure to become the last steam railway owned by British Rail, finally being privatised in 1989.

Steam motive power did survive in BR service elsewhere – but only in the form of self-propelled steam cranes, some of which remained in use into the 1980s.

Nobody seriously expected a new steam engine would one day bring multitudes flocking to the lineside, like the excited short-trousered schoolboys of the 50s when the gleaming new Standards appeared, to see it in action.

Tornado would defy those non-expectations in the biggest way possible.

Chapter 5

FROM TALYLLYN
TO *TORNADO*

The last British main line steam locomotive appeared half a century ago, after which the facilities needed to build them were closed down. So how is it that a group of ordinary people who were drawn together by a common dream of re-creating one of Peppercorn's masterpieces, were able to do it?

It is ironic that just two years after the appearance of the first Peppercorn A1, a nationwide movement began that would one day be able to build a brand new one

Gresley A3 Pacific No 60103 Flying Scotsman at King's Cross station in 1963, just before its last journey to its Doncaster birthplace and sale to enthusiast Alan Pegler. It is now owned by the National Railway Museum at York, which was officially opened by the Duke of Edinburgh in 1975 and is considered the focal point of the UK heritage railway movement. NATIONAL RAILWAY MUSEUM

The plight of locomotive No 2 Dolgoch in 1949 led to the Talyllyn Railway being saved by volunteers and thereby launching the railway preservation movement, which now has the building of a new A1 at its pinnacle. ROBIN JONES

– outside an established railway workshop, without grant aid and without any involvement by British Railways.

The roots of the railway preservation movement can be traced back to late summer 1949 when fears were sounded for the survival of the independently owned Talyllyn Railway after No 2 *Dolgoch,* its sole operational locomotive, suffered a fractured frame and was withdrawn from service.

It seemed certain that the little 2ft 3in gauge line would soon share the fate of its close neighbour the Corris Railway, which had been closed down by British Railways shortly after it inherited it from the Great Western Railway at nationalisation in 1948.

Renowned transport author Tom Rolt wrote a letter to *The Birmingham Post* in the summer of 1950, arguing that rather than ask "why don't they do something about it?" people who wanted to save the line should get stuck in themselves.

The line's owner Sir Haydn Jones died on 2 July that year, and while his widow kept services running until the end of the summer season on 6 October, it then appeared that it had closed for good.

Following Rolt's letter, a public meeting to consider the future of the Talyllyn was held on 11 October 1950 at the Imperial Hotel in Birmingham, and 36 people turned up. A committee was elected, and on 23 October, meeting for the first time, it adopted the name of the Talyllyn Railway Preservation Society.

On 27 September 1825, the Stockton & Darlington Railway became the first in the world to run public steam-hauled passenger trains. Its first locomotive was 0-4-0 Locomotion No 1, built in George and Robert Stephenson's works under Timothy Hackworth. A very early subject for preservation, it is now displayed in Head of Steam – Darlington Railway Museum, a stone's throw from Tornado's birthplace. ROBIN JONES

Pacifics were being built for tourist use in Britain 82 years before Tornado appeared on the main line. The Romney, Hythe & Dymchurch Railway has eight in its fleet, including No 3 Southern Maid, built by Davey Paxman in 1926. **ROBIN JONES**

Volunteers were recruited, many from the West Midlands area, and after acquiring two locomotives from the Corris Railway, restored services on the Talyllyn at Whitsun 1951. They were the first trains to be run on a railway that had been preserved by enthusiasts, as opposed to a line built by enthusiasts for pleasure purposes.

Today, there are well over 100 private railways in Britain which offer steam journeys. Virtually all of them owe a debt of gratitude to the Talyllyn pioneers, who faced ridicule in trying to preserve steam at a time when there was no real threat to its existence.

Back in 1950, saving a steam engine was seen by many as like someone today trying to preserve a modern Volkswagen car straight out of a showroom for the distant future when the type would no longer be made.

So why bother? Britain had just seen the appearance of 49 gleaming new A1 Pacifics, and between 1951 and 1960, British Railways would turn out 999 of its new Standard steam locomotives. The demise of steam seemed light years away.

Preserving railway artefacts was, however, far from being a new concept: indeed, the Edaville Railway in South Carver, Massachusetts, began operating in 1948 on part of a redundant 2ft gauge system which had served a cranberry bog using some of the original locomotives and stock, and therefore claimed the title of the world's first preserved railway. However, in many ways, the Edaville railway was an artificial

The first preserved steam locomotive to haul the Royal Train on the main line was Princess Coronation Pacific No 6233 Duchess of Sutherland, seen leaving Holyhead on 11 June 2002 with the empty stock en route to Llandudno. This locomotive survived the scrapyard because it was one of several bought out of British Railways service for static display at Butlins holiday camps. BRIAN SHARPE

GWR 4-6-0 No 6000 King George V, seen on display in the STEAM museum in Swindon, ended the British Rail steam ban in 1971, paving the way for steam locomotives to run over the national network again, and therefore much later for a new A1 Pacific to be built for the main line. ROBIN JONES

museum-style creation of rich enthusiast and cranberry magnate Ellis D Attwood as opposed to a 'genuine' historic public line like the Talyllyn.

The first steam locomotive to be preserved was *Invicta,* which ran on the Canterbury & Whitstable Railway until it was withdrawn in 1839. At first displayed in a public park, it is now exhibited in Canterbury Heritage Museum.

The next engine to be saved for future generations was *Locomotion No 1,* one of the pioneers from the Stockton & Darlington Railway, which was set aside in 1857 and is now displayed in Head of Steam, the revamped Darlington Railway Museum next door to *Tornado's* birthplace at the former Hopetown carriage works.

The preservation of a handful of early pioneer engines helped establish a principle whereby obsolete locomotives could become worthy museum pieces. Several major railway companies preserved a few examples of classic traction. The most famous example from the 19th century is, of course, Stephenson's *Rocket,* which is now displayed in the Science Museum in London.

Naturally, there were many landmark locomotives which were not saved for posterity, but which in historical terms would now be considered priceless. For instance, nothing remains of Richard Trevithick's locomotive, which gave the world's first public demonstration of steam haulage by rail along the Penydarren Tramroad near Merthyr Tydfil in 1804.

The big event of 1925 was the cavalcade to mark the centenary of the opening of the Stockton & Darlington Railway. The LNER saved several locomotives that otherwise might have been scrapped so they could take part in the procession, and that continued with the subsequent saving of Atlantic No 251 and No 990 *Henry Oakley*. Because of this action, the LNER is reasonably represented today in terms of pre-Grouping types. A major spin-off was the decision to save these locomotives for posterity, establishing a railway museum at York, which later became today's National Railway Museum.

The debate over what should have been set aside from the railway network for future generations rather than be allowed to pass into oblivion has raged for decades – and indeed, has been one of the prime driving forces behind the public support for *Tornado*.

Redundant railway locomotives and rolling stock in museums have always been objects of fascination. It is impossible to tell exactly when schoolboys first became fascinated by passing trains; but if you were to hazard a guess at the years immediately following the dawn of steam, you would probably not be far wide off the mark.

Toy trains became popular in Victorian times, although they were little more than crude toys that bear no relation to today's finescale model railways. However, there were those who realised that miniature trains had a fascination of their own, one which could generate tidy profits – if you sold them to wealthy enthusiasts, or invited the public to pay to ride on them.

The plethora of seaside miniature railways which graced the promenades and parks of virtually every major British resort at one stage may be traced back to a 15in gauge line built by landowner Sir Arthur Heywood on his Duffield Bank estate in Derbyshire in 1874, with the aim of selling it to a wider audience. In 1895 he built such a system at Eaton Hall in Cheshire for the Duke of Westminster. This particular line drew the attention of one Wenman Joseph Bassett-Lowke, who was to become the most famous model maker of the early 20th century.

Bassett-Lowke was already familiar with a passenger-carrying miniature line at Blakesley Hall near Towcester, which linked the mansion to the local railway station, using two imported Cagney Bros US-style 4-4-0 steam locomotives.

With the aid of engineer Henry Greenly, Bassett-Lowke formed a company, Miniature Railways of Great Britain, in 1904, to market the concept.

The first venture was the acquisition of an existing 10¼in gauge line from the Bricket Wood Railway at St Albans, which Bassett-Lowke installed next to Northampton's Abington Park, opening at Easter 1905.

Many a rich enthusiast yearned to drive his own locomotive, but of course any railway company would have been automatically horrified by any such proposal. Bassett-Lowke, however, enabled such dreams to be fulfilled. Thus the principle of a public railway line, albeit a miniature one, which was owned, managed and driven by enthusiasts, was established.

The Severn Valley Railway began running public services in 1970 and is today Britain's second most popular heritage line in terms of passenger numbers. Visitors Gresley LNER V2 2-6-2 No 4771 Green Arrow and GWR 4-6-0 No 4936 Kinlet Hall are seen in gala action in September 2007. BRIAN SHARPE

While conflict raged on the Western Front in 1915, Bassett-Lowke turned his attention to the derelict 3ft gauge mineral-carrying Ravenglass & Eskdale Railway in the Lake District, which he saw advertised for sale following its closure to passengers in 1908 and freight in 1913. The line, which ran for seven miles from Ravenglass into the Cumberland hills, had been England's first public narrow gauge railway when it opened in 1875.

Bassett-Lowke bought it and relaid it to 15in gauge, introducing miniature locomotives, scaled-down versions of main line prototypes, and turning it into an attraction.

He then switched his attention to central Wales and a 2ft gauge horse-drawn tramway, which carried passengers from the *Bannouth* ferry on the south side of the Mawddach estuary to the seaside village of Fairboume, which had been opened in the 1890s to serve a brickworks. He converted it to 15in gauge and reopened it in 1916 as the Fairbourne Railway.

In both cases, Bassett-Lowke had gone beyond building a miniature railway for either a private estate, seafront or park for amusement. These two lines became public passenger-carrying railways in their own right, had been developed on the trackbeds of previous lines, both of which had been used for purposes other than tourism, and had been revived with the enthusiast in mind.

Miniature railway aficionado Captain JEP Howey, whose family had made a fortune from the development of Melbourne in Australia, built the Romney, Hythe & Dymchurch Railway and opened it in 1927. Billed as the world's smallest public railway, it was also a 'main line in miniature' using Pacifics to haul trains over double track which eventually extended to 13½ miles. Built by an enthusiast for enthusiasts, yes; but at the time this railway could not be considered as heritage, because not only was it brand new but also it was simply mirroring the state of the art in locomotive design on the full size main line at the moment.

Moving several strides forward, the now familiar concept of local people rolling their sleeves up to run a railway, without pay if necessary, had its roots in the closure of the 3ft gauge Southwold Railway in Suffolk in 1929. Two alternative schemes appeared: one involving a consortium of local councillors and moneymen; while the other was proposed by the line's former locomotive engineer, who wanted to convert it to standard gauge. Neither scheme won enough support; and further bids also failed, the railway finally being scrapped for the war effort in 1942.

It was therefore left to the Talyllyn Railway to perform the 'big bang' which launched the start of the volunteer-led rail revival movement.

At the time, however, it was more of a whimper than a bang. In 1951, Dr Richard Beeching and his infamous axe were still a dozen years into the future, and most of the British Railways branch line closures of the 50s had not even been announced, so there were comparatively few lines for others to save.

For many, the Talyllyn was an overnight success, for also in 1951, a meeting in Bristol led to the formation of a society to reopen the much bigger 1ft 11½in gauge Ffestiniog Railway.

The idea of rail revival by ordinary folk hit the big screen in 1952 when 1838-built Liverpool & Manchester Railway locomotive *Lion* starred in the Ealing comedy *The Titfield Thunderbolt,* which, with startling clarity of future vision, told of efforts by a local community to save their closure-threatened railway.

In 1954, businessman Alan Pegler obtained a controlling interest in the Ffestiniog Railway company; and the following year, the first section, between Porthmadog and Boston Lodge was reopened to passengers by volunteers.

A few years passed before revivalists began looking at saving standard gauge lines too. Added impetus for such moves came in the British Railways Modernisation Plan of 1955, which demanded the speedy replacement of all steam.

In 1958, a group of Leeds University students under the helm of their lecturer Dr Fred Youll formed a trust and took over the running of the Middleton Railway, a private industrial line which claimed to be Britain's oldest railway in continuous service, having run since 1758. That year, the Lincolnshire Coast Light Railway at Cleethorpes became the first new line in Britain to be built by enthusiasts, using stock reclaimed from industrial systems in the county.

Just like the old days: the Ffestiniog Railway turned out a second brand new double Fairlie, David Lloyd George, in 1982. It is seen running along the deviation beyond Dduallt, a route which was hacked out of the mountainside by volunteer labour in the 60s, with the old trackbed visible below. FR

New wine in an old bottle: Earl of Merioneth, the modern double Fairlie built by the Ffestiniog Railway in 1979 to a basic design that was by then well over a century old. This locomotive kick-started the building of new locomotives by the preservation movement, although it would be 30 years before one would take to the main line. FR

The replica of the broad gauge Iron Duke outside the National Railway Museum. NATIONAL RAILWAY MUSEUM

The Southwold Railway so nearly became Britain's first preserved railway, but it would be another 22 years after its closure in 1929 before volunteers were able to run their own steam trains on the Talyllyn. ROBIN JONES COLLECTION

In 1959, the Bluebell Railway Preservation Society was formed. It was the first organisation to take over a section of a closed section of the British Railways network, in this case part of the Lewes-East Grinstead route.

In 1960, the Bluebell and Middleton railways ran their first passenger trains, leading, incidentally, to an endless debate as to which one had been the first to do so.

The year before, Captain Bill Smith VRD, RNVR had become the first private individual to buy a locomotive from British Railways, in the form of Great Northern Railway/LNER J52 0-6-0ST No 68846, latterly King's Cross shed pilot engine.

The year 1961 saw the formation of the Scottish Railway Preservation Society, while four schoolboys, irate that a Collett 0-4-2 auto tank was not included in the British Transport Commission's approved list for steam locomotives to be saved as part of a National Collection, banded together to set up the Great Western Society, which eventually established Didcot Railway Centre.

The snowball begun by the Talyllyn was now gathering more substance, and further volunteer-driven revival schemes were launched – the Dart Valley Railway on the GWR Ashburton branch, the Severn Valley Railway at Bridgnorth, the Welshpool & Llanfair Light Railway and the Keighley & Worth Valley Railway in Yorkshire. The latter became the film set for EMI's big-screen version of the Edith A Nesbit classic *The Railway Children*, which prompted masses of vital publicity for the nascent preservation movement.

The decades that followed saw yet more revival schemes: the West Somerset Railway, Britain's longest standard gauge heritage line at 24 miles; the Great Central Railway at Loughborough, the world's only standard gauge double track heritage trunk railway; and the North Yorkshire Moors Railway, the most popular of them all in Britain, carrying more than 300,000 passengers a year and in the 21st century having extended regular services over Network Rail's Esk Valley line from Grosmont into Whitby; the East Lancashire Railway, the North Norfolk Railway, the Gloucestershire Warwickshire Railway and many more.

In 1963, Ffestiniog saviour Pegler bought no less a machine than Gresley A3 Pacific No 4472 *Flying Scotsman* from British Railways, and used it on a main line special just three months later. Just why a record breaker like *Scotsman* was not earmarked for the National Collection is beyond belief; had it not been for Pegler's prompt action, it may well have been an A3 that a future generation would have to build to fill a missing gap in the country's heritage fleet, rather than an A1.

The common theme of all these achievements is the little man taking on the big boys and showing that he can do as well if not better than the powers that be.

For not only did the revivalists save lines from closure (and even if they could not restore regular public services as first hoped, they turned them into popular tourist attractions) but in the six decades that following the rescue of the Talyllyn, worked many miracles well over and above their call of duty to achieve their goals.

One of the first such mountain-moving feats was no less than that – moving a mountain, or as near to it as you could get. After the Ffestiniog Railway closed,

Yorkshire's Keighley & Worth Valley Railway is one of the great preserved lines and has been saved in its entirety. LMS 'Jinty' 3F 0-6-0T No 47279 is seen crossing Mytholmes viaduct in October 2008. BRIAN SHARPE

plans were made to flood part of the route for a reservoir to power a hydro-electric power station.

The Llyn Ystradau reservoir cut the line in half, and it would have been so easy for the revivalists to settle for less.

However, they were determined that nothing would stop them reconnecting Porthmadog Harbour station to the eastern terminus of Blaenau Ffestiniog once more, and so they spent years hacking a new route out of the slate mountainside to bypass the reservoir, even creating a spiral loop to allow the railway to gain height in the process. In volunteer terms it was nothing short of a marvel in engineering; no less commendable was the legal battle for compensation, which took 18 years and two months, the second longest in British legal history, before victory was attained in 1972. At last, on 25 May 1982, Ffestiniog trains ran into Blaenau again.

In 2009, the year that *Tornado* made its public debut on the main line, the Ffestniog completed another marvel – the rebuilding of the original Welsh Highland Railway linking the north coast of Snowdonia to the south. Linking to the Ffestiniog via a tram-like town section, the two lines together now offer a 40-mile steam highway from Caernarfon to Portmadog and Blaenau Ffestiniog. Including the stunning Aberglaslyn Pass, it is without a doubt one of the finest railway journeys anywhere in the world, yet without the early revivalists, would have been lost forever.

Yet what of the locomotives that provide motive power for preserved lines?

In the early days, preservation schemes could buy engines straight out of service from British Railways, but after steam on the main line ended with the 'Fifteen Guinea Special' on 11 August 1968, that was no longer possible.

As they were withdrawn, steam locomotives were sold by British Railways to local scrap dealers, who usually cut them up without delay.

One big exception was Woodham Brothers scrapyard of Barry Island in South Wales. Proprietor Dai Woodham decided one day that cutting up old wagons and coaches was more profitable than dismantling steam engines, and took a far-reaching decision to leave the latter rusting in long rows in the Bristol Channel air for years.

It was a decision made on commercial grounds, but it allowed the railway preservation movement enough time to gather sufficient strength to reach the point where it was able to buy and restore the rusting hulks, even though some of the projects took 25 years or more to complete. In all, a total of 213 steam locomotives were bought from Dai Woodham for preservation purposes, and again, many miracles were performed in rebuilding them.

Tales of such projects abound, but special mention must be given to the 71000 Duke of Gloucester Steam Locomotive Trust, which in 1975 dared to do what other preservationists baulked at – restore the moribund rusting wreck that was *Duke of Gloucester.*

The unique 8P Pacific was withdrawn in 1962 and ended up at Barry. Unlike other Barry survivors, it was incomplete, having had its outside cylinders removed, sectioned and displayed at the Science Museum in London.

Not only did the trust's members rebuild No 71000, but, incredibly, made the modifications that would have seen it attain its full potential in British Railways days, before the modernisation plan scuppered any such aim.

Back on the main line, its achievements were manifold, such as the fastest ascent to Ais Gill on the Settle to Carlisle line in 1991, four years later beating both Princess Coronation Pacific No 46229 *Duchess of Hamilton* and streamlined A4 60007 *Sir Nigel Gresley* in trials over Shap on the West Coast Main Line, and recording the fastest recorded climb of Camden Bank by steam, attaining 41mph with the equivalent of 13 coaches behind it.

Another key milestone had been passed. Not only were scrap locomotives being returned from the graveyard to continue where they left off, but the evolution of main line steam was being continued by preservationists. The heritage sector showed that in this field, it could be pro-active as well as passive.

The downside of Woodhams' benevolent scrapyard in terms of saving what in just a few years' time would become regarded not as rusting hulks but priceless historical artefacts, was its location. It was top heavy with Southern and Western Region classes, with few rusting locomotives from other parts of the system. So today's heritage fleet has an imbalance: we have 30 Bulleid Pacifics, for instance, but no LNER B17 Sandringham 4-6-0 or Great Eastern Claud Hamilton 4-4-0. These types were sent to locomotive graveyards in their own locality where reclamation of scrap was immediate. Only one LNER locomotive emerged from Barry, in the form of Thompson B1 No 61264.

The wider implication of the Barry factor is that the collection of heritage locomotives we enjoy today may be entertaining, but it is by no means a fair or accurate representation of British railway history. While several locomotive types are abundant in preservation, others are glaringly absent. Falling into the last category was – until now – a Peppercorn A1 Pacific.

British Rail slapped a ban on steam locomotives on the main line – *Flying Scotsman* excepted – after 11 August 1968. Following sustained pressure from the heritage sector, that ban was lifted in autumn 1971 when, following trials, GWR flagship 4-6-0 No 6000 *King George V* headed a 'Return to Steam' special from Hereford to Tyseley via Newport and Didcot on 2 October 1971, hauling a rake of Pullman coaches painted in the livery of owner the Bulmer Cider company.

That paved the way for a select number of preserved main line engines to return to the national network to haul special trains, and so steam was once again no longer restricted to private lines.

In 1994, an East Coast Main Line landmark was passed when Gresley A4 No 60009 *Union of South Africa* became the first of its class for 30 years to run out of King's Cross, hauling a special organised by Flying Scotsman Services.

It has been estimated that the volunteer army running Britain's heritage railways and museums stands at around 22,000, and if they laid all the lines together, they would exceed the length of the West Coast Main Line from London to Glasgow.

Once a particular group's chosen line was back up and running, new goals were set. Some lines extended, while others concentrated their efforts into honing infrastructure to perfection. Eventually, some groups looked at the imbalance in the portfolio of surviving steam locomotives, and wondered – would it be feasible to plug the missing gaps?

The Ffestiniog Railway led the way yet again. Back in 1869, George England built *Little Wonder,* the first double-ended Fairlie patent articulated 0-4-0+0-4-0T for the tightly curving line. The type became synonymous with the line, and with the reopening to Blaenau approaching, the line needed new motive power. So a century later, in 1979, at its Boston Lodge workshops, the railway built a brand new double Fairlie, *Earl of Merioneth,* based on the original concept, although with modern box-like side tanks. Another double Fairlie, one of a more traditional appearance, *David Lloyd George,* followed in 1992, and filling the gap left by the scrapping of the original locomotive, a replica single Fairlie 0-4-4T *Taliesin* followed in 1999. Taking shape in the same workshops for several years has been *Lyd,* a replica of original Lynton & Barnstaple Railway Manning Wardle 2-6-2T *Lew.*

In April 1847, the first of Daniel Gooch's Iron Duke 7ft 0 ¼in ground-breaking broad gauge express passenger 4-2-2s, *Iron Duke*, emerged from Swindon Works. None survived, but in 1985 a fully working replica was built using parts from two standard gauge Hunslet Austerity 0-6-0 saddle tanks, specially for the Great Western 150 celebrations. It is now in the National Railway Museum.

It is a logical train of thought to ask – if we can build replica narrow and broad gauge steam locomotives, then with half a century of preservation experience and skills backing us up, why can we not tackle a lost standard gauge type?

Enter The A1 Steam Locomotive Trust and *Tornado*.

Chapter 6

A NEW A1 FOR THE
PRICE OF A PINT!

lthough one had the benefit of 40 years' preservation experience on the
other, there were striking parallels between the launch of the Talyllyn
Railway rescue and the project to build an A1.

Both were born as a direct consequence of like-minded people coming together
through correspondence in a newspaper column. In the case of the Talyllyn, it was
The Birmingham Post; with *Tornado,* it was the now-defunct enthusiast weekly
Steam Railway News. In the late 1980s, enthusiast Mike Wilson of Stockton became
involved in a bid to elevate the status of the town's railway station to reflect its
historic importance on a global stage. During one campaign meeting, it was

The public launch of The A1 Steam Locomotive Trust at the Railway Institute in York on 17 November 1990.

suggested that a cosmetic replica of a locomotive could be built to go on display there. It could even be a replica of an A1….

The A1 Steam Locomotive Trust's headboard.

Also in the 80s, preserved steam locomotive engineer Ian Storey of Morpeth cast his eye over the spare boiler, cylinder block and tender for *Flying Scotsman,* then based at the former Steamtown museum at Carnforth, Lancashire, and pondered with colleague Richard Campbell as to whether they could form the basis of a project to recreate an A1. Finally, another enthusiast, David Champion, had been mulling over the idea of a new-build main line Pacific since the mid-60s, after becoming infuriated by a magazine article in which it was argued that the best way to preserve steam engines for posterity was to model them.

David said to his brother Phil: "No it's bloody not! The best way is to build brand new steam engines; and mark my words, someday people will start building new main line steam locos to replace the one's now being preserved – they can't go on running forever."

He recalled: "The former LNER main line was a racing ground for the Pacifics of Gresley, Thompson and Peppercorn. More than any other region, you were likely to see a Pacific on a main line passenger train. Oh how we loved them. They were powerful, handsome, and each class had its own identity as a distinctive family of engines.

"You can best understand the depth of this bitter loss by thinking what it would be like for you as a teenager if the Beatles were taken away from you in 1965."

Biding his time, David watched with interest Mike Satow's building of replica locomotives from the dawn of steam and the new Ffestiniog double Fairlies. David said: "I noted the advances in expertise of the heritage movement as it found a way to cast new wheels, cylinders, manufacture new fireboxes, boilers, smokeboxes, valve gear, just about every component that was needed for a brand new engine, but they were manufactured to keep an existing engine running. By the late 1980s, everything that could be done to preserve main line steam had been done, including the restoration to steam of No 71000 *Duke of Gloucester.* That restoration has involved the manufacture of so many new components that many recognised that the next step must be to build an entire new locomotive, albeit to an old design.

The magic spark flew in April 1990. Mike Wilson proposed in the weekly newspaper *Steam Railway News* that an organisation be launched to build a brand new fully-fledged A1 Pacific. Avidly reading his words were the Champion brothers.

"We realised intuitively that this was the point where we stopped being onlookers," said David. "If the generic 'they' wouldn't build brand new main line engines, we would have to do something about it ourselves."

The brothers wrote to Mike offering to join the project. Several others had also expressed an interest, but an initial meeting attracted only a few of them, and some lost interest within a few months and drifted away.

The project instigators hoped to follow the example of the many preservation societies that existed by then, but David realised that far more money and business expertise would be needed for a mammoth project like the building of no less than a new Pacific, if the scheme was ever to make headway.

Mike replied: "Look, I haven't got that sort of experience, but you are in business – could you put it together?"

David agreed and recruited Ian Storey and Newcastle-upon-Tyne lawyer Stuart Palmer, a former colleague who he had bumped into at the previous year's North Yorkshire Moors Railway steam gala.

He agreed to come on board, and in spring 1990, the four people who would become the founders of The A1 Steam Locomotive Trust sat around the dining table of David and his wife Gillian at their home at Espley in Northumberland. David, Mike, Ian and Stuart decided to launch the project in York by the end of the year. The National Railway Museum confirmed that most of the A1 drawings still existed. Ian estimated that the project would cost £1-million at 1990s prices. The big question was – not could an A1 be physically built, but could such a small group raise that sort of money?

David mulled over the problem day and night for many weeks. "It needed to be a new slant on raising money," he said. "It needed to have the right professional organisation to manage the money, the marketing, administration and the build.

"As the largest single project ever attempted, it would need the best of current business practices and a culture of excellence if people were to believe in it enough to give their money. I had to be able to show right from the start that all that was necessary to succeed was in place, but up to that point all we had was wishful thinking."

One evening in August 1990, he finished off a bottle of particularly good red wine in his study and ideas for fundraising came fast and furious. He wrote them all down – and still has the sheet of A4 paper to this day. He also realised that it was not enough to build a replica A1 Pacific. It had to be the next A1 Pacific, the 50th member of the class. That simple decision gave a licence to make small changes to the original design, while remaining demonstrably faithful to the greater part.

When the group met again the following month, David outlined his strategy. "A million seemed a huge target, but if we made it obligatory that everyone who contributed made covenants into a charitable trust, contributions would be grossed up by the taxman, who would effectively fund 25 per cent of the locomotive. So the mountain instantly reduced in size.

The Tornado project may not have been drawn up on the back of the proverbial beermat, but it has been built for giving the price of a pint – each week since 1990! Back then, beer cost £1.25 a pint in the North East!

"Then I said that if we just tackled it one step at a time, the going would be easier – just as with eating an elephant. If that is the job in hand – the way to do it is to eat a little each day."

He produced a sheet of paper which showed simply a picture of a pint of beer. He told his astonished colleagues: 'I will show you how we are going to build this engine for the price of a pint of beer.'

If enough people gave the price of a pint of beer a week on a regular basis, the money raised could pay for a new A1. "Large numbers of people meant it would get built quicker, less covenantors and it got built slower – but it still got built."

David fed stories into the local press, while Phil launched a project newsletter, and 120 people packed out a meeting at the Railway Institute in York on 17 November 1990. So great was the attendance that people were standing on the stairs outside. Ted Parker gave an audio-visual presentation entitled 'Visions of A1s' before the team outlined the strategy. It was revealed that the new locomotive would be numbered 60163, the next in line of the class under the British Railways numbering system.

David then publicly signed the first covenant – and was greeted by an ovation.

Within half an hour, 100 people had also signed up including Wreford Voge, an accountant and expert on charities from Edinburgh. Subsequently several top quality professional people offered their services, including Barry Wilson, then vice-president of Bank of America in Jersey, was welcomed on board, followed by aero industry engineering David Elliott, marketing man Mike Fanning from Doncaster and, marketing and PR expert Mark Allatt . They were later joined by experienced project planner Rob Morland and then Andrew Dow, the previous head of the National Railway Museum.

David succeeded Mike Wilson as trust chairman, a position he held for 10 years, before his wife became terminally ill with cancer. "We had 10 wonderful, stressful, hyper-busy years with the A1 project, and we had over 50 tons of new A1, including frames, wheels, cylinders and cab, sitting in our new locomotive works at Darlington, with new pieces being manufactured steadily," he said.

The last of the A1s, No 60145 St Mungo, is seen being broken up in 1966. Accordingly, a line of preserved East Coast Main Line motive power from the 1890s until the end of steam was thus broken by the absence of a Peppercorn A1. A1SLT

Redrawing the A1 Blueprint

That crucial early support at the Railway Institute meeting meant that the project was a goer. The starting point would later see a wheel turn full circle. While in 2008 the completed *Tornado* would be unveiled at the National Railway Museum at York, it was here that the initial stages of the project began in the early 90s.

It was at this stage that the planned locomotive acquired its name, after the fighter bomber that helped crush Saddam Hussein's forces in the first Gulf War of 1991.

Having ascertained before the launch of the project that many drawings for Peppercorn A1s had been saved from Doncaster Works when it stopped undertaking steam overhauls, in 1993 the painstaking job of cataloguing, scanning, cleaning up and redrawing them began.

The A1 Trust's technical team, by this time led by David Elliott, spent several weeks at the museum establishing exactly what drawings had survived.

Ultimately, around 95 per cent of the original drawings were discovered. These were mostly Indian ink tracings on linen.

Around 1100 drawings were scanned in 1993 followed by a further 140 in 2001. These were then electronically deskewed and cleaned.

However, a few had to be completely redrawn due to the poor quality of the originals.

Many of them have been subsequently modified or redrawn to add material specifications and tolerances to make sense of such steam era gems as 'this bolt to be a good fit' and 'this item to be made with special care' and ascertain exactly what 'best Yorkshire iron' actually is!

Best Yorkshire Iron was indeed described in LNER Specification No 41 of August 1939, but no copy of such a specification has been found. It was a sure bet that such a material was no longer available.

OPPOSITE TOP: A representative from RAF Leeming presented The A1 Steam Locomotive Trust officials with a print of a Tornado F3 fighter and received a picture of a the future completed Tornado at Darlington Locomotive Works on 16 March 2002. DAVID ELLIOTT/A1SLT

BOTTOM: A Royal Air Force GR4 Tornado Multi-Role Combat Aircraft releases flares during a combat mission over Iraq in 1991. Ironically, Tornado's director of engineering David Elliott came from a background in the aircraft industry.

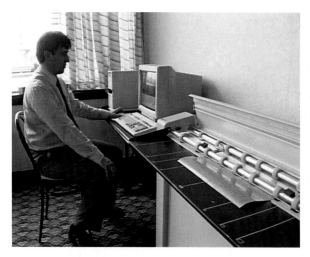

David Elliott operating the drawing scanner at the National Railway Museum in York in 1993. A1SLT

David Elliott and team checking A2 measurements at NRM, York in 1993. 1 April 1993. TED PARKER

One of the many original Peppercorn A1 drawings in the National Railway Museum archives at York. NATIONAL RAILWAY MUSEUM

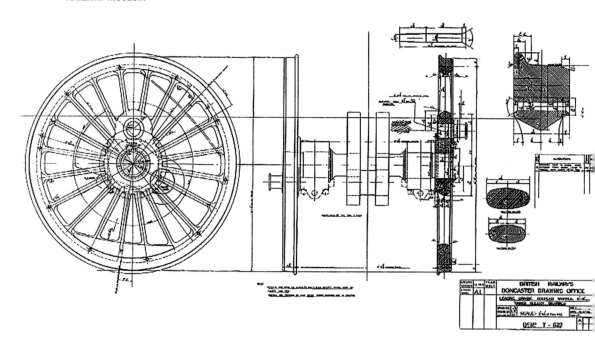

Cutting the frames

The physical construction of the locomotive started, logically enough, with the manufacture and erection of the frames.

Here, there was the first of the big differences between the 50th A1 and the originals.

As David Elliott explained: "We used a single plate frame instead of spliced frames. The originals had each frame plate in two pieces with a lap joint about 4ft over the leading couple axle.

"We never truly found the reason why. The most plausible argument was that at the time these were being built, there was a national shortage of steel and all the biggest bits were going to shipyards that were building ships for export, so the domestic requirements fell secondary. So there was some pressure to make use of

Dorothy Mather, with Bob Meanley, admires progress of Tornado's frames at Tyseley Locomotive Works in December 1994. ROB MORLAND/A1SLT LIBRARY

Side plates for Tornado's frames after cutting at BSD Leeds. BRIAN BATE/A1SLT LIBRARY

The completed frames at BSD in 1994. A1SLT   **The frames being cut in 1994. A1SLT**

smaller plates, and therefore by using spliced construction you needed less length in the steel plates.

"I'm not sure how valid that is, but bearing in mind that virtually all the pre-war engines were built with single plates, we made a decision to go down that route.

"That is the biggest single change and the consequence of it is that the inside cylinder block is 2½in narrower and 1⅛in wider on each side than the original, to kept the pistons in line with the connecting rods."

"It is only someone with a tape measure who would notice."

Typically, the frames are made of plate steel, and were cut out as a pair by a computer-controlled machine at the new BSD (now part of Corus) facility in Leeds.

The machine was started by Dorothy Mather, the widow of Arthur Peppercorn, who had graciously agreed to become the A1 Trust's president, thereby providing a unique continuity between the steam age and the present day.

The cutting of the frame plates was the first of many ground-breaking events covered extensively by both newspapers and TV as well as the railway press.

The frame plates were the subject of the first major sponsorship agreement for the trust with BSD securing unprecedented press coverage for the opening of its new facility. They have since been described as the most accurately made plate frames ever applied to a steam locomotive.

Then it was time for the frame stretchers.

On the original A1s, the frame stretchers were cast and at the front end the middle cylinder in effect becomes a massive frame stretcher of enormous strength. This manufacturing process was fine when building a batch of 49 but very uneconomic when producing just one locomotive.

The A1 Trust therefore utilised the modern method of using polystyrene as opposed to traditional wooden patterns, at around a third of the cost, for simple 'one off' castings; and occasionally substituted welded fabrications for castings.

It had originally been hoped to build the new A1 at Doncaster, from where Nos 60114-60129 and 60153-606162 had been outshopped, and talks were begun with the local council about finding a permanent engineering base.

However, the talks collapsed. The decision was taken to erect *Tornado's* frames at Birmingham's Tyseley Locomotive Works, which back in the late 60s had become one of the pioneering preservation sites thanks largely to the efforts of the late Pat Whitehouse and his colleagues.

Under modern-day chief mechanical engineer Bob Meanley, Tyseley has become a centre of excellence for the maintenance and operation of steam locomotives on the main line, primarily Great Western types. It would be Bob who would oversee the erection of *Tornado's* frames.

The polystyrene pattern for the frame stretcher. A1SLT

The cutting of the frame plates. A1SLT

Next come the Cylinders!

Thanks to a substantial donation by a covenantor, the Trust was able to embark upon the complex process of making the cylinders.

The cylinders represented a huge challenge for the patternmaker, who was brought out of retirement specially and spent 12 months working to produce enough woodwork to fill a small pantechnicon!

With no steam era railway workshop left in Britain to help, the Trust resorted to using multiple suppliers – Kings Heath Patterns of Cotteridge, Birmingham, British Steel Engineering for the castings (again now a part of Corus and done on very favourable terms as an apprentice project) and Ufone Engineering, now of Dudley, West Midlands, for the machining.

And to the surprise of the covenantors and supporters at the trust's spring meeting at Tyseley Locomotive Works in 1996, the trust's president Dorothy Mather was able to unveil *Tornado's* three cylinders to the cheers of those present.

Machining the three cylinders, which were largely financed by a covenantor's donation. A1SLT

Assisted by the then chairman David Champion, Dorothy Mather unveiled Tornado's three cylinders to the cheers of those who attended the A1 Trust's spring meeting at Tyseley in 1996. ROB MORLANDS/A1SLT LIBRARY

The A1 Trust's second chairman and Tyseley Locomotive Works Chief Mechanical Engineer Bob Meanley lean out of the cab of No 60163 at Tyseley in 1997. A1SLT

Hopetown Lane Carriage Works, on the route of the world's first public steam-operated railway, the Stockton & Darlington, and the place where Tornado was built, taking steam engineering in the town proudly into a third century. DAVID ELLIOTT/A1SLT

Tornado's frames pass Trowell Junction, Nottingham, en route to going on exhibition at the National Railway Museum in York in March 1997. BOB NEWITT/A1SLT

Tyseley's contribution had been second to none, but since the collapse of talks with Doncaster Council, the Trust had been looking for an appropriate permanent home in which to complete the erection of *Tornado*.

In 1995, the borough council in Darlington, where the remaining original A1s had been built, came to the rescue with the offer of the old Hopetown Lane Carriage Works near the town's North Road station at an appropriate 'Peppercorn' rent!

Again, Trust president Dorothy Mather was on hand to receive the ceremonial key from the council leader.

Following the award of £300,000 in grants from the European Regional Development Fund, the National Heritage Memorial Fund and Darlington Borough Council in 1996, work started to convert the derelict building into the new Darlington Locomotive Works where *Tornado* would come together, stage by stage, and the trust moved in during 1997.

A locomotive's identity is said to derive from its frames, essentially its backbone around which all other components are arranged.

So it may be held that *Tornado's* first main line outing came in March 1997, after the new Darlington workshop was ready.

Following the completion of the main frames at Tyseley, including the fitting of the three cylinders and six horn blocks, *Tornado* began its journey to its new home in Darlington via the National Railway Museum in 1997 on the back of an EWS freight wagon.

The semi-completed locomotive was displayed for several weeks in the Great Hall.

By then, the Trust's principal sponsor had come on board – William Cook Cast Products Ltd.

The frames on display inside the National Railway Museum in 1997. A1SLT

The Wheels and Motion

William Cook Cast Products Ltd, a large UK-based engineering company, started as a steel casting manufacturer and evolved to the point where today it produces sophisticated components, assemblies and systems for a huge range of applications.

When company chairman Andrew Cook read an article about the A1 Trust in *Professional Engineering* magazine, he contacted David Elliott with an offer of help. This led initially to the company casting *Tornado's* six 6ft 8in driving wheels on 'very advantageous terms' at its Burton-on-Trent plant in Staffordshire. This agreement, which allowed the trust to make a monumental leap forward and bring forward the completion of *Tornado* by several years, was later extended to all of the wheels on the locomotive.

The first wheel was cast in 1995, and as principal sponsor, William Cook has since helped out with almost every steel casting on *Tornado.*

The company's William Cook Rail subsidiary is now recognised for its specialist manufacture of steel castings for steam locomotives, including driving wheels, horn blocks, frame stays, cylinders, blast pipes and superheater headers. Its manufacturing facilities allow the firm to produce such components as single items without difficulty or extreme cost.

Incidentally, William Cook Rail is today also the owner of the French steam locomotive No 141R 568, built in 1945 by Baldwin Locomotive Works in the

The forging of Tornado's motion at John Hesketh & Son Ltd of Bury.
FASLINE PHOTOGRAPHIC/A1SLT

Coupled wheelset after wheel pressing at Riley & Son (Electromech) Ltd, Bury, with Ian Riley and the crew. DAVID ELLIOTT/A1SLT

United States and sent to Europe as part of the Marshall Aid plan for the reconstruction of France.

Only six survive in working order today – four in France and two in Switzerland – and the William Cook Rail locomotive is unique in being the only coal-fired 141R still in operation, carrying the traditional black and red livery.

Following the company's deep involvement with *Tornado,* it bought the 141R locomotive in France in 2005 and moved it to Switzerland for overhaul the following year. It is operated on behalf of William Cook Rail by the Swiss steam train and museum association, Vapeur Val-de-Travers, which owns and preserves one of the largest collections of standard gauge, main line steam locomotives in Switzerland.

William Cook Rail has assembled a 10-car train of historic Swiss carriages to run behind its 141R. Titled the William Cook Classic Train, it will be available for charter for corporate events and tourist excursions both in Switzerland and beyond.

The company's involvement in heritage steam extends beyond railways. It has played a major role in the re-engineering of the paddle steamer *Montreux* which operates on Lake Geneva.

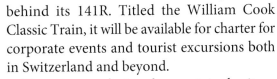

The fitting of the motion at Darlington Locomotive Works. DAVID ELLIOTT/A1SLT

Trailing wheelset during balancing at Dowding & Mills in 2007. A1SLT

A moveable feast at last: the wheelsets in place beneath Tornado's frames in November 2000. ROB MORLAND/A1SLT

While the Cook castings were undoubtedly first class, the lack of a recognised major railway workshop again formed an obstacle to progress on *Tornado*.

The lack of a fully equipped 'plant' meant that the already complex assembly of the wheelsets was made even more difficult due to the need to do related work at engineering sites many miles apart.

Tornado's wheels were pressed onto their axles at heritage steam locomotive engineer and owner Ian Riley's Riley & Son (Electromech) Ltd works in Bury, Lancashire.

The procedure took place after David Elliott and his team undertook a bout of 'industrial archaeology' to discover just how it was done on the original roller-bearing engines – because nothing was written down on the original A1 drawings.

Surprisingly the lubricant of choice for the pressing operation was Tesco's own brand of rapeseed oil!

Tornado's driving wheelsets spent much of 1999 and 2000 shuttling up and down the M6 between Bury and the Severn Valley Railway's workshops in Bridgnorth.

By this stage, most of the major heritage railways had evolved to the point whereby they had developed significant engineering facilities of their own.

The Bridgnorth works is equipped with a lathe capable of turning *Tornado's* 6ft 8in driving wheels both before being fitted with their tyres and again after they had been shrunk on. The wheelsets were delivered to Darlington Locomotive Works in July 2000 and first placed under the locomotive's frames in time for the November 2000 Trust covenantors' convention.

The process of completing the wheelsets started in 1995 with the casting of the first wheel at the Burton plant of William Cook Cast Products Ltd and continued right through until 2007 when their balancing was carried out. A1SLT

Tornado's wheels and motion are turned at Darlington in 2004. A1SLT

Machining of motion components. DAVID ELLIOTT/ A1SLT

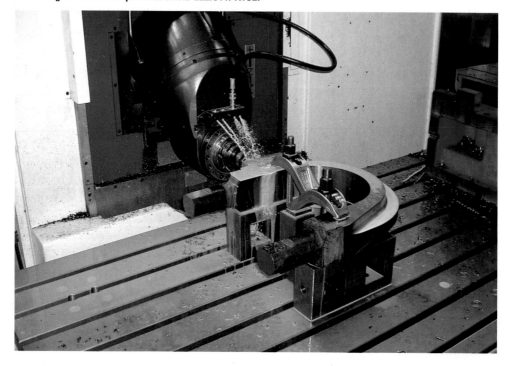

Tornado's 6ft 8in driving wheels being turned at the Severn Valley Railway's workshops in Bridgnorth. DAVID ELLIOTT/A1SLT

This first set of driving wheels for a main line steam locomotive since 1960 had taken five years, used nine suppliers and cost approaching £100,000 to get this far – even allowing for the generosity of William Cook Cast Products Ltd sponsorship.

Attention then switched to *Tornado's* motion.

Its forging proved to be a long and expensive process, with costs totalling around £50,000.

The majority of components were forged by John Hesketh & Son Ltd of Bury, a firm that, sadly, has now closed leaving a critical gap for the heritage railway movement.

The motion project began with the manufacture of the slidebars in 1999 and finished with the inside radius rod in 2002.

Suppliers used included Ufone Precision Engineering Ltd, Multi-Tech Engineering of Featherstone and I D Howitt Ltd of Crofton and cost more than £100,000.

The fitting of the motion to *Tornado* involved considerable adjustment and trial fitting due to the fine tolerances associated with a roller bearing-fitted locomotive.

The inside cylinder motion was finally completed in early 2008, when the valve setting took place.

The Boiler

With many new-build locomotive projects, the biggest and most expensive component is the boiler. Cab sides and roofs, smokeboxes and smokebox doors and frames may look impressive when recruiting supporters, but they are very much towards the cheaper end of the parts list. Raising the finance to build a boiler is therefore the acid test of whether such a project will succeed. The A1 Trust took the decision to separate the construction of the boiler and smokebox due to the long lead time and complexity of both the engineering and the funding of the former.

The barrel was rolled by a sponsor and the door done as a project by supporter Ian Howitt. The almost complete smokebox was first fitted to the locomotive in 2000.

Covenantors arrived at the trust's annual convention at Darlington in October 2002 to be greeted by a shape which very much resembled a Peppercorn A1, albeit in skeletal form, but able to move on its wheels for the first time.

Draped between the smokebox and a cab was a banner appealing for £350,000 to fill the gap where the boiler should be. So how was the trust to fund this out of an income that by September 2005 had reached £10,000 per month?

The nearly complete smokebox at Darlington in 2000. DAVID ELLIOTT/A1SLT

Director of Engineering David Elliott addresses trust supporters at the annual convention in October 2002, when work on the locomotive was sufficiently advanced for Tornado to move on its wheels for the first time and attention now started to turn to the boiler.

Such a flow of funds is very convenient for the manufacture of large assemblies which have a multiplicity of parts in a wide cost range. However, it does not suit the acquisition of large single assemblies that must be bought from a single supplier in one piece at one time, such as the boiler. The choice was stark. The Trust could sit and do nothing while income accumulated in the bank, or could seek new income from covenants, launch a bond issue whereby investors would be repaid within a set period of years plus interest, or take out a commercial loan.

The last option was found to be unavailable to the Trust – because at the time there was no locomotive, and therefore nothing to offer as security!

However, there was no doubt as far as the supporters were concerned: money should be raised on the financial markets to bring forward the completion of *Tornado* by several years.

Accordingly, the Trust launched a £500,000 bond issue in 2004. But where would such a big boiler be available in the modern era, nearly 40 years after the last British Railways main line steam ran? And what type of boiler would it be?

The boilers fitted to the original A1s were all-riveted constructions, with copper fireboxes. A decision was made to replace the copper firebox with a steel version,

Cramped maybe, but who's complaining? A1 Trust officials including its third chairman Mark Allatt, operations director Graeme Bunker, director of engineering David Elliott, finance director Barry Wilson, Duncan Ross, director of administration and quality and certification director Graham Nicholas squeeze inside the firebox in Meiningen in 2006. A1SLT

primarily because of the cost saving. However, once such a decision was made, the trust was plunged into redesign territory, and any redesign had to be approved before manufacture could commence. The same principle applied to the decision for the boiler to be welded rather than riveted.

The Trust therefore had to seek a boiler manufacturer who had a proven design capability as well as relevant manufacturing capacity.

Director of Engineering David Elliott explained: "The reasoning behind what we've done with the boiler is that the likelihood of finding a modern pressure vessel manufacturer who would build us a traditional riveted boiler with a copper firebox was not very good. The modern industrial boiler manufacturers all use all-welded boilers with steel fireboxes.

"We had hoped in the early days that we might get significant sponsorship from one of these manufacturers. That didn't come

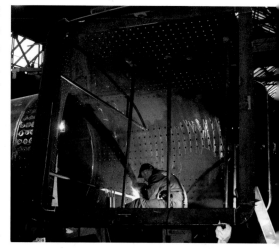

A view inside Tornado's firebox in Meiningen Works. A1SLT

The completed boiler for Tornado being unloaded on Sunday 16 July 2006 following its journey from Germany.
KEITH DRURY/A1SLT

about, but when the time came that we had to press on with the boiler, we approached over a dozen boiler and pressure vessel manufacturers in the UK.

"We got positive bites from two who, unfortunately due to the receding nature of the boiler industry in the UK at the time, within the first year of discussions with each of them had rationalised their design capabilities so they felt they could no longer support us.

"This caused us to push that particular enquiry further afield and approach four outlets in Europe. Three took some interest and two, one in Poland, one in Germany, took considerable interest, and at Dampflokwerk Meiningen (Steam Locomotive Works Meiningen) in the former East Germany we found a resource that was just streets ahead of anything else we had seen.

"Uniquely it had the capacity to design and build all at the same works."

Following a thorough procurement process in February 2006, the trust announced that it had placed the order for the boiler with Meiningen, then a workshop of the Deutsche Bahn (the German Federal Railway).

This followed on from an initial order for the redesign of the original LNER Diagram 118 boiler which was completed in August 2005 with construction of the boiler commencing in October 2005.

In June 2007, the completed boiler for Tornado was lifted onto the rolling chassis at Darlington Locomotive Works, marking another major milestone in Tornado's construction. DAVID ELLIOTT/A1SLT

Other redesign work had to be undertaken in conjunction with the boiler. Network Rail asked that the height of the locomotive be reduced by one inch to 13ft to meet modern safety requirements for running under electrified wires. On the boiler, this inch had to come from the dome and the mounting of the safety valves.

"The A1s were originally designed at 13ft 1in which until about 2000 was the go-anywhere loading gauge for BR and subsequently Railtrack," said David Elliott. "In 2000 Railtrack brought out a new proposed standard which reduced the maximum height for the go-anywhere loading gauge to 13ft. This was never formally converted into group standards but on the strong recommendation of our

The modification of the structure of Tornado to accept two air pumps and air brake cylinders. DAVID ELLIOTT/A1SLT

It took two attempts to get the casting for the superheater header right. DAVID ELLIOTT/A1SLT

Vehicle Acceptance Body we reduced the height of everything on the loco to 13ft or less.

"It has had a useful side effect in that as far as I'm aware, we have had no restrictions anywhere on the East Coast Main Line due to clearance of electric wires and when we went out on the Southern, we had no bridge clearance restrictions, whereas other locomotives do in certain places. So the extra inch has helped.

"We've done it in such a way that it's only when you see *Tornado* standing next to A2 Pacific No 60532 *Blue Peter* that it's obvious that it's a bit lower. It's surprising that it makes *Blue Peter* look an inch taller."

Tornado's boiler was completed by Meiningen on schedule in June 2006, and a successful hydraulic test was undertaken on 10 July 2006.

It was witnessed by not only the Technische Überwachungsverein, a German notified body, the Trust's Vehicle Acceptance Body and boiler inspector, but also members of the British and German press.

Six days later, *Tornado's* complete boiler was unloaded at Darlington Locomotive Works using a 200-ton crane.

There were, as expected, many who refused to believe during the progress of the *Tornado* project that the day would come when it would steam. When the boiler arrived, most of those doubts evaporated.

Tornado was now very much on the home straight.

Work then became focused on the preparation of the frames to receive the boiler and the cladding for the boiler. This work included the modification of the structure to accept two air pumps and air brake cylinders, large sized pipework and the painting of the area between the frames in red. By June 2007 work was sufficiently advanced to enable the boiler to be fitted to the frames.

The completed boiler, with its new cladding temporarily removed, was lifted onto the locomotive's rolling chassis at Darlington using a 100-ton crane.

In November 2007, the superheater header successfully passed its hydraulic test and was subsequently fitted to the locomotive.

The Final Assembly

With the boiler under way, the trust turned its attention to the last remaining major part of the locomotive on which work had not yet begun – the tender. Again, Andrew Cook, chairman of William Cook Cast Products Ltd, generously offered to help.

In July 2005 the Trust announced that his firm, its principal sponsor, would now also be sponsoring the construction of the £200,000 tender with work ongoing in parallel with the completion of the locomotive.

The countdown to steaming was now on!

Due to space constraints at Darlington Locomotive Works, it was decided that ID Howitt Ltd of Crofton, Wakefield, would erect the tender frames off-site at its workshops.

The contract for the construction of the tender tank was let to North View Engineering Ltd of Darlington. By December 2007 it was complete and ready for mounting on its frames. It had to wait for the fitting of the brake cylinders, air, steam heat and vacuum pipe work, air receivers, electrical conduit and terminal boxes and Train Protection & Warning System apparatus aerial bracket to the tender frames before it could be lowered onto them.

The new A1 takes shape big time inside Darlington Locomotive Works in July 2007. A1SLT

The tender tank at North View Engineering Ltd of Darlington. DAVID ELLIOTT/A1SLT

The tender is another part of *Tornado* that has been modified from the original Peppercorn A1 design to better equip the locomotive for operations on today's main line railway.

The tank has been redesigned internally, eliminating the water scoop, increasing the water capacity from 5000 gallons (22,700 litres) to 6200 gallons (27,240 litres) and reducing coal capacity from 9 tons to 7 ½ tons.

In December 2007 the tender frame arrived at Darlington from ID Howitt's workshops to be united with its wheels for the first time. From the outset, the trust intended that *Tornado* would run on the main line at speeds compatible with today's traffic. It was therefore vital that full certification was obtained.

A derogation (No 05/0150/DGN) was issued against locomotive 9883 (8P 4-6-2 locomotive No 60163 *Tornado*) exempting the new Pacific from the need to comply with a range of Railway Group Standard requirements.

Many of these exemptions are similar to those granted for existing steam locomotives approved to run on the UK network. They include such aspects as exemption from the need for a diesel-style front end yellow warning panel or a crashworthy 'crumple zone'.

Miles and miles of pipes: the countdown to steaming has involved the fitting of what seems like miles and miles of steam, oil and air piping. DAVID ELLIOTT/A1SLT

Tender frames take shape at ID Howitt Ltd, Crofton, Wakefield, in May 2006. NIGEL FACER/A1SLT

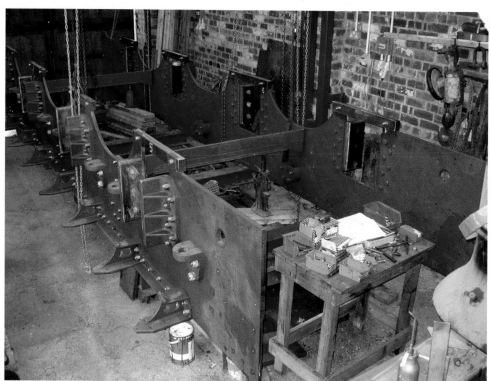

The tender tank nearing completion. DAVID ELLIOTT/A1SLT

Issue of the derogation allowed the process of design certification to be completed, confirming that the locomotive complied by design with the remaining applicable Railway Group Standard requirement.

The certification subsequently allowed the remainder of the Vehicle Acceptance process to go ahead, ultimately resulting in the issue of a certificate of Engineering Acceptance.

The Engineering Acceptance certificate is used to gain Network Rail route acceptance and HM Railway Inspectorate approval, which then allows the locomotive to enter service on the national network.

The speedometer waits to be fitted. A1SLT

Tender frame and wheels united! DAVID ELLIOTT/A1SLT

As part of the certification process, the trust had to manage and record every aspect of the manufacture of *Tornado* to ensure that this is possible within current certification and inspection requirements for motive power operating on Network Rail. As part of this process, a series of trials was booked for the Great Central Railway.

Director of engineering David Elliott explained: "Back when we started, British Rail (subsequently followed through by Railtrack and Network Rail) laid down a condition that if we built to the original design, we would not have to do design scrutiny on each individual component. The argument was that the A1s ran for 16 years and produced some figures showing that they were among the most reliable and cheapest to run of all the Class 8 Pacifics around on British Railways, so the basic design was sound.

"Other changes have been brought about by the need to make the engine comply with modern safety systems and standards.

"We have fitted air brakes to the loco. The original one had steam brakes on the loco and vacuum brakes on the train, but because we were starting with a clean sheet of paper, it was fully air-braked.

"We have a vacuum ejector and vacuum control so we can still haul vacuum stock on heritage railways but steam brakes have been eliminated altogether.

"Furthermore, to comply with modern regulations, we needed to do a lot about the electrics on the loco.

"Although the original A1 had a very simple turbo generator providing electricity for lights on the loco, it was not a very satisfactory system and we needed a much more dependable form of electricity to drive modern saftey equipment.

"Among the modern safety gear we had TPWS, On-Training Monitoring and Recording apparatus and NRN Radio (National Radio Network, historical British Rail radio which is still in use). We have a need in the future to fit the new GSMR radio, which is a high-security derivative of mobile telephone technology; and to that extent, with the installation we had put on the loco for NRN radio, the box is big enough for us to tear the NRN radio out and fit the GSMR radio in the same space later, so we have done a bit of future proofing.

"Steam locomotives for electricity almost invariably rely on batteries which are charged off the loco and taken on for each trip, or are charged in situ

"We made a decision early on that with the quantity of electrical equipment we now have to fit plus to give us capacity for the future, it would make sense to put more charging on the loco.

"So in addition to batteries, we have two sources of charging while we are going along. One source is a coach alternator that we took off a former TPO sorting van and the other one is a turbo alternator, which we bought from Meiningen where they have modified the traditional German turbo alternator by fitting a Bosch truck alternator, 28v, which enables you to charge batteries off it. The original design of 25v was not enough to charge a battery off it.

Looking like a 'real' locomotive: Tornado awaits its boiler cladding. A1SLT

"The other reason why we decided to go for a high integrity on-board generation system was that it has two independent battery systems on it. This has come about because I spent 17 years in the aircraft industry and that's the way that aircraft do their electrics. But a crucial thing here is that we expressed an interest in doing 90mph on a regular basis. And one of the key requirements of 90mph is that we have permanent fixed headlamps.

"The portable headlamp that is used by most steam locomotives on the main line is approved only up to 75mph. As soon as you go on to the fixed headlamps, the group standard requires that you have security of supply. In addition to a battery, you need a generator.

"That pointed the trust down the route of on-board generation so that we fully comply with group standards. As a result of some very good work by a colleague of one of our trustees, who works for a technology company around Cambridge, we now have fully group standard compliant headlamps with LED lamps in them that actually fit into traditional oil lamp casings.

"The lights, which were originally fitted to the A1 locos, have been modified with LED bulbs in them, red and white switchable from the cab, so there again they are fully group standard compliant with switchable bulb failure warning lighting up in the cab to let us know whether the thing is on or not."

Paperwork and delays in getting the final small components made left Trust officials and supporters straining at the leash to see their locomotive in steam 'straight out of the box'.

Christmas 2007 came – and they would not have to wait for much longer…

The First Fire

The first fire in Tornado inside the works, the smoke from the chimney throwing the rays of sunshine into profile.

Sunlight and smoke: Darlington Locomotive Works had finally come of age as the first fire was lit inside Tornado. ROBIN JONES

TOP LEFT: A proud Dorothy Mather inside a very smoky Darlington Locomotive Works after the first fire was lit on 9 January 2008. ROBIN JONES

TOP RIGHT: Beaming with delight was an understatement for A1 Trust chairman Mark Allatt's reaction to the first steam being emitted from Tornado. ROBIN JONES

LEFT: Coal is shovelled in by former Doncaster premier apprentice Malcolm Crawley, vice president of the A1 Trust. ROBIN JONES

OPPOSITE PAGE: Helped by A1 Trust operations director Graeme Bunker, Dorothy Mather tips the first lighted rag into the firebox of the new A1. ROBIN JONES

The author helps push Tornado out of the works. MAURICE BURNS

Eighteen years of talking, fundraising, making parts big and small. Yet no sign of smoke. That is until 9 January 2008, when 56 years after the death of the A1's designer Arthur H Peppercorn, his widow Mrs Dorothy Mather ceremoniously tipped the first pieces of coal into the firebox of No 60163.

In front of a low-key assembly of invited guests at Darlington Locomotive Works, a circle was thereby completed; a direct lineage between the glorious steam age of the past and the new steam era of the 21st century.

The event preceded the lighting of the first fire inside *Tornado,* even though the locomotive was still not ready to move under its own power.

Delays in completing the last vital components plus the urgency for more fundraising would delay that historic moment for another frustrating six and a half months.

Nonetheless, to see steam pouring from the chimney for the first time was, for many, including Dorothy, the magical moment.

It was the first time since *Evening Star* was outshopped from Swindon Works in 1960 that a fire was lit in a new steam locomotive built for the UK national network.

A1 Trust chairman Mark Allatt declared: "The lighting of the first fire is tremendous news for *Tornado* and the future of main line steam in Britain.

"There is no more appropriate person than Dorothy Mather to carry out this ceremonial task as she is the widow of Arthur Peppercorn."

The shafts of light from the harsh afternoon sunlight through the high windows of the locomotive works were thrown into sharp relief by the steam slowly but surely filling the workshops, in a scene reminiscent of countless engine sheds across the world on a daily basis for a century and a half.

Eventually, *Tornado* was pushed out of the shed by an eager band of volunteers, every roll of the wheels turning another page in transport history.

Following the lighting of the first fire, the boiler was slowly warmed for two days, building up steam to enable it to reach its operating pressure of 250lb/sq in.

The operation was overseen by representatives from the trust's Notified Body, Delta Rail, and boiler inspector John Glaze, before *Tornado* was awarded its 10-year boiler certificate.

The race then began to complete the final assembly of the locomotive and tender as rapidly as possible.

Mark said: "When this project was launched in 1990, many people said that it could not be done. The steaming of *Tornado's* boiler proved the doubters wrong."

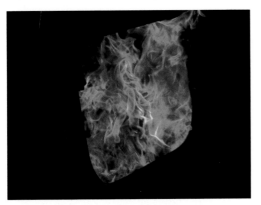

The first fire inside Tornado. ROBIN JONES

The chimney sees use for the first time. ROBIN JONES

No smoke deflectors yet, but the first wisps of smoke float into the blue Darlington sky. ROBIN JONES

All it needs is the smoke deflectors: Tornado inside Darlington Locomotive Works on 18 July waiting to turn a wheel in anger. A1SLT

Chapter 7

THE FIRST PASSENGERS

At the start of August 2008, the same month that Britain marked the 40th anniversary of the end of steam on British Railways, the first new steam locomotive built for service on the national network in 48 years moved under its own power for the first time.

Transport history was made at Darlington Locomotive Works on Friday 1 August when, in the presence of Dorothy Mather, *Tornado* moved under its own power along the 120 yards of running line.

At the helm was operations director Graham Bunker with fireman Chris Duckers assisting with the shovel.

The steaming staged for the national press came four days after *Tornado* moved for the first time during a preliminary trial at Darlington. After all, the trust had to make sure it all worked before inviting the world's press!

The media launch rewarded the trust with a concoction of headlines across the world and TV exposure.

Tornado's first movement along the short running line outside its birthplace was proudly witnessed by the trust's three chairmen, Mike Wilson, David Champion and Mark Allatt, current holder of the post.

Mark Allatt and Mrs Dorothy Mather. ROBIN JONES

Gauges inside the cab during the demonstration run. ROBIN JONES

Citing 18 years of criticism since the small group of enthusiasts drew up the idea of building an A1 in 1990, Mark said it all: "This is the one they said would never run."

The weekend immediately afterwards allowed the covenantors who donate a set amount of money each month to see *Tornado* in action for the first time.

Few words could express the sheer delight of seeing an 'impossible dream' finally coming true; the grey bulk of the out-of-the-box A1 enshrouded in pure white smoke as it reversed from the door of the Hopetown Lane workshop to the buffer stop at the boundary fence and returned again.

Finally, the weekend of 9-10 August saw the public being allowed into the works to see *Tornado* move.

The Mayor of Darlington, Coun Ian Haszeldine, climbed aboard for a footplate ride, and described it as 'an experience of a lifetime'.

He added: "Very few people get the chance to do this. I've looked forward to it for a long time and thoroughly enjoyed it. It was absolutely superb.

"There was a big queue of people waiting to get on the train. It just goes to show the interest, not

Graeme Bunker, the A1 Trust's operations director, smiles from the footplate. ROBIN JONES

Tornado moves for the first time in public, at the press preview day at Darlington Locomotive Works on 1 August. ROBIN JONES

Dorothy Mather waves from the cab of Tornado. BRIAN SHARPE

Accumulating light engine mileage on the Great Central Railway, Tornado passes Woodthorpe Lane on 23 August.
BRIAN SHARPE

Making an appearance at the Thomas weekend, No 60163 comes off shed at Loughborough on 24 August 2008.
BRIAN SHARPE

just in Darlington but also nationally in this project."

The date was certainly poignant, for 11 August was the 40th anniversary of the 'Fifteen Guinea Special' which marked the end of steam haulage of passenger trains on British Railways.

Days later, that long and winding road from the fledgling preservation movement in Tywyn in 1949 led to Loughborough, completing a railway circle spanning 130 years. It was in 1878 that Hughes Locomotive & Tramway Engineering Works Ltd of Loughborough supplied an 0-4-0ST for use on the Corris Railway, and it was later converted to an 0-4-2ST.

After the Corris was closed by BR, the little engine was bought by none other that the Talyllyn revivalists, and was named after the line's late owner, Sir Henry Haydn Jones. As the line's No 3, it went on to become a mainstay of motive power, as the Talyllyn volunteers showed everyone else that 'it could be done'.

It was as if the heritage movement of the 21st century had brought a far, far bigger offering to repay a debt of gratitude.

Tornado, moved by haulage contractors Alleyly's, was offloaded at Quorn & Woodhouse on the Great Central Railway, Britain's first double track heritage main line, on the morning of Wednesday 20 August.

From there, it was towed to Loughborough Central by humble Class 08 diesel shunter D4097.

Of course, with a brand new Peppercorn A1 on a double-track railway and a team of builders itching to see what it could do, there was no way on earth it was going to stay locked up in the shed. Later that same afternoon, final adjustments were made and a fire was lit inside the A1.

It moved from the shed and posed for photographs alongside the platform at Loughborough.

On the Thursday, *Tornado* completed two light engine runs down the line and back.

One of the big attractions of the Great Central for the A1 Trust was that not only

The world's media scramble for their pictures of the first public movement of Tornado of Darlington on 1 August.
ROBIN JONES

would it give their locomotive the chance to stretch its legs, but it could also undergo 60mph testing with a line possession order. The railway is one of the few independent lines in the country to be allowed to run locomotives at that speed, under strict conditions.

However, *Tornado's* arrival had already produced 60mph running, but not as intended. Some lineside photographers had heard rumours that it was to haul a train on the Friday; and when that did happen, they chased it at that speed both along country lanes and even in at least one station car park.

That day, the A1 took a trip to Rothley, hauling the line's LMS directors' saloon to ensure that the locomotive's vacuum ejectors and brakes worked. *Tornado* propelled the coach back from Rothley to Loughborough.

David Champion, the second chairman of the A1 Trust, was on board the first train, with his dog Bud wearing a 60163 jacket!

Former chairman David Champion at the fireman's window as *Tornado* heads the second train of the day taking A1 Trust supporters on their first rides behind *Tornado*, near Woodthorpe on the Great Central Railway on 20 September 2008. RAY PETTIT/A1SLT

Once back at Loughborough, the line's headquarters, *Tornado* sidled up to the Great Central's seven-coach dining train, coupled up and took it as an empty coaching stock movement all the way to Leicester North.

The sight of the train passing all the familiar landmarks and photographic vantage points so beloved by enthusiasts and regular visitors to the Great Central was yet another pinnacle reached; yet another peak conquered by a movement which has been made up of ordinary people who have time and time again since 1949 proved their determination to keep Britain's world-beating transport heritage alive and vibrant despite the disinterest of the authorities of the day, who allowed so much of it to be swept away.

The Saturday saw *Tornado* take somewhat of a sideways move. The Great Central was holding a Thomas the Tank Engine event, and although it was not built when the late Reverend Wilbert Awdry wrote the books, *Tornado* entered into the spirit of the occasion with a face added as it stood outside Loughborough shed. Perhaps its 'new' identity was as a distant relative of Gordon the Green Engine, which the author based on an LNER locomotive.

Not only that, but *Tornado* also completed two light engine trips down the line, again with the plastic face on – another first for the A1 class! On the Sunday, *Tornado* ran another trip to Leicester North with coaching stock, and on Bank Holiday Monday, it was coupled to its first goods train. By the end of the weekend, the locomotive had 150 miles on the clock.

Another press day was arranged for 26 August, this time for the *Daily Mail* and Tyne-Tees TV, and the following day, the trust's Vehicle Acceptance Body inspector visited Loughborough to check *Tornado* over.

Tornado rests on Great Central metals after delivery by Allelys Haulage to Quorn & Woodhouse on 20 August. BRIAN SHARPE

Raw power of an A1: Tornado waits to haul its first load of passengers from Quorn & Woodhouse on 21 September 2008. ROBIN JONES

It also underwent an inspection by HM Railway Inspectorate, hauling 11 coaches and a 'dead' Class 45 Peak diesel, the week before it hauled its first passenger-carrying trains. That happened on Sunday 21 August, when around 1000 covenantors and their guests were allocated seats in an exclusive train undertaking several round trips of the whole length of the line from Quorn & Woodhouse to Loughborough, south to Leicester North and back to the midway starting point; and so at last were able to proudly ride behind No 60163 for the first time.

With the first trip departing at 10.15am, the locomotive, still in its grey undercoat with the trust's website address on the sides of the tender, hauled an eight-coach train, including the award-winning restored LNER Beavertail saloon.

It was the first passenger train hauled by the A1 since it was delivered to the line; and it was allowed after HM Railway Inspectorate gave approval the previous week, following a loaded test run. Among the VIPs on board were past Trust chairman David Champion, whose dog Bud wore a coat with 60163 sewn into it!

In the superb sunshine and summer-like temperatures on the first day of autumn, crowds gathered both on the station platforms and overbridges to glimpse history being made.

All the trips went faultlessly, and nobody on board had anything but utter admiration for *Tornado* and the team that built it at Darlington.

It is 5pm on 24 August 2008, and Tornado heads another empty stock train out of Loughborough Central. BRIAN SHARPE

Tornado enters Quorn & Woodhouse after bringing its empty coaching stock from Loughborough. ROBIN JONES

Tornado runs round its train at Leicester North. ROBIN JONES

The following day, the railway offered the public the chance to ride behind *Tornado* for the first time.

And Monday 22 September, *Tornado* hauled scheduled ordinary public passenger service trains for the first time.

Great Central Railway president Bill Ford enthused: "This is a terrific honour for the GCR. *Tornado* has been the talk of the railway enthusiast community for years; but now it's finally ready to run, the whole world is taking notice."

Testing of the A1's On-Train Monitoring Recorder (OTMR), Train Protection & Warning System (TPWS), Automatic Warning System(AWS), all mandatory for runningany main line locomotive in the 21st century, and air brakes took place while *Tornado* was at the Great Central Railway.

Three weeks later, on 10-12 October, *Tornado* – still in its grey 'undercoat' – took top billing for what was hailed as the most successful steam gala held by the modern-day Great Central Railway in its 39-year history.

Around 7000 passengers travelled in seven-coach trains packed to standing room only, while every vantage spot from roadsides and overbridges was packed by spectators. At one point on the Saturday, police closed the road leading to Quorn & Woodhouse station as so many cars were queuing to get into the site.

In traffic, *Tornado* was joined by the National Collection's BR Britannia Pacific No 70013 *Oliver Cromwell,* returning to the line where it underwent a four-year overhaul; Southern railway 4-6-0 No 850 *Lord Nelson* and LMS Jubilee 4-6-0 No 5690 *Leander.*

A special guest was His Honour Edgar Fay QC, the son of legendary original Great Central Railway general manager Sir Sam Fay, who celebrated his 100th birthday from the comfort of the dining train. Fay Senior ran the GCR between 1902-23.

The beer tent entered the spirit of the event with four specially brewed ales – Tornado, Cromwell, Nelson and Leander! However, the LMS brew was the first one to sell out.

Tornado, which had by then completed several 60mph runs on the line and had clocked up its first 1300 miles by the end of the event, not only hauled passenger services, but also took its place on the line's Travelling Post Office train and 'windcutter' rake of mineral wagons.

Tornado enjoyed its first taste of small screen stardom in the days following the gala.

A 30-minute documentary about the A1 project, *Absolutely Chuffed: The Men Who Built A Steam Engine*, was shown on BBC4 on 16 October 2008 and repeated three days later on BBC2 on Christmas Eve.

Tom Ingall, co-producer of the programme, who is also the GCR's press officer, said: "This has been a fascinating project. From the moment I first saw the A1 under construction, it was clear there was a great deal of passion and pride involved – invested over so many years."

Chapter 8

UNDER COVER OF THE NIGHT…

Tornado reached the Great Central Railway on the back of a lorry, and also left it via a low-loader. However, the A1 Trust said it would be the first and last time that the locomotive would be transported in this way. Visits to everywhere else would from then on be made by only one way – rail.

Following the completion of the running-in and trials on the heritage railway, the timehad come for the most important tests of all – on the national network.

It would be these that would finally decide whether 18 years of hard graft had been worth it – or in vain.

Tornado was duly delivered to the National Railway Museum at York for the trials to begin.

The first trip, from York to Scarborough on the evening of 4 November, saw No 60163 and a support coach reach speeds of 50mph.

The run was deliberately not advertised beforehand, yet news spread like wildlife along the unofficial lineside 'grapevine'.

Such was the fame that *Tornado* had by now acquired, even when it was still in its coat of grey primer, that hundreds turned out in the dark to catch a first glimpse of it speeding by.

Chairman Mark Allatt said he was taken by surprise by the additional national media interest that the first test run had generated, over and above the previous extensive coverage afforded to *Tornado* in previous weeks following its completion and running-in on the Great Central Railway.

"We were covered in the free Metro which was distributed all over the country, and we had our fifth big feature in the *Daily Mail*," he said. "We had a double-page spread in the same issue that the results of the US election were being analysed, and certainly not an easy day on which to get such big coverage."

Two days later, *Tornado* undertook its 60mph non-passenger carrying loaded test run, hauling a rake of 12 ex-Virgin Trains Mk2 coaches with a 'dead' Class 67

Turning a wheel in steam on the main line for the first time, A1 Pacific No 60163 Tornado heads slowly through platform 4 at York station en route for Scarborough with its support coach on 4 November. Alongside is a National Express Class 91 electric locomotive, which is much older than the steam locomotive. BRIAN SHARPE

Tornado stands in Newcastle central station after the first leg of its 75mph test run from York on 18 November. BRIAN HURST

As National Express is the modern-day inheritor of the route for which the Peppercorn A1s were built, it was fitting that the company should sponsor its final test run, prior to which, Tornado is pictured outside the National Railway Museum at York, the logo on its tender. DAVID ELLIOTT/A1SLT

Tornado departs Platform 5 for Scarborough on 6 November. BRIAN SHARPE

Tornado passes Bolton-on-Dearne on its York-Sheffield test run on 6 November. ANTHONY SKIPWORTH

The final coats of apple green paint being applied to Tornado's driving wheels inside the National Railway Museum's paint shop by Ian Matthews on 8 December 2008. ROBIN JONES

Nearly ready to go: an 18-year dream is set to come true as Tornado awaits its official launch just days away.
ROBIN JONES

diesel No 67026 on the end, from York to Sheffield and Barrow Hill and back, equating to a load of 550 tons.

At one stage, *Tornado* hit 75mph for the first time.

On return at York, small traces of white metal were found on an upper crosshead. "It ran a bit hot due to indifferent lubrication," said Mark. "We have corrected the problem by taking the crosshead off and providing enhanced lubrication to the upper slider.

"This is exactly what test runs are for, so we can discover these things before the locomotive enters main line service."

Mark added that he was amazed by the size of the crowds that turned out, particularly at York and Sheffield stations. Following rectification of the crosshead problem, *Tornado* undertook a light engine run in the week on 17 November, to ensure that all was well prior to its second and 75mph loaded test run the following day.

Unusually, *Tornado*, still in its grey 'livery', carried the logo of trip sponsor National Express, the operator of electric services on the East Coast Main Line, on its tender for the return trip from York to Newcastle.

It was fitting that the 50th A1 carried the livery of the contemporary main operator on the East Coast Main Line, just as the first 49 had worn the apple green adopted from the LNER, whose last Chief Mechanical Engineer designed them.

Setting off from York with its first full-size main line train, No 60163 leaves platform 10 at York for Sheffield on 6 November. BRIAN SHARPE

Director of engineering David Elliott said: "We had a couple of issues during our trials with problems with crossheads, the first of which was down to a lubrication problem which we eventually traced down to a modification.

"We had built all the gravity lubrication systems to the original drawings and I failed to notice that there was a note on one of the original drawings dated 1955 which had increased the bore of the little siphon tubes in the oil boxes from ¼in to ⅜in. That suggested that they were having lubrication problems in the early days.

"As soon as we modified all our siphon tubes to ⅜ the problem with intermittent shortage of oil went away.

"We also had problems with another crosshead but that was down to a manufacturing problem with the white metal not having been applied properly."

Apart from these very minor problems there was little doubt from its first main line outings under cover of darkness that *Tornado* richly deserved its main line ticket.

'Effortless' was the word used by Trust operations director Graeme Bunker in summing up the locomotive's final proving run from York to Newcastle-upon-Tyne on the evening of 18 November.

Hauling 10 mostly empty coaches (there were guests on board) plus a precautionary Class 67 in case of breakdown, the 4-6-2 hauled its load of 425 tons along the East Coast Main Line with ease, reaching sectional line speeds with power to spare.

Such was the excitement on board the train that English Welsh & Scottish Railway chief engineer Phil Johnson was overheard to say: "We could use a fleet of this type of engine!" Riding as a guest, heritage main line tour operator Steam Dreams' Marcus Robertson – a self confessed follower of Southern as opposed to LNER steam – described *Tornado's* run as 'extraordinary'.

"Apart from the sound of the exhaust I heard nothing from the front end which one normally experiences when a locomotive is working hard," he said. "In fact I didn't get the usual sensation that the train was steam hauled – it was that quiet.

"Indecently," he added. "It was quite a thought that the accompanying Class 67 diesel was much older than the locomotive at the front.

"*Tornado* certainly reaches the parts that other engines have not."

All that now remained before *Tornado* would haul its first public trips on the 'big' railway was for its livery to be applied.

That took place in early December, when No 60163 *Tornado* was painted in BR apple green and lined out, with BRITISH RAILWAYS spelt out in capital letters on the tender.

For once, transport history was not merely conserved at the National Railway Museum in York, but made, for the transformation of the locomotive from grey primer to the livery carried by the first 30 of the 49 original A1s back in 1948 took place in the paint shop.

The painting was undertaken by the father-and-son team of Ian and Dan Matthews of M Machine (which had previously applied the grey livery at Darlington) with Tony Filby, the museum's painter, applying the lettering and Mike Tompson the lining.

The apple green paint was donated by Wordsley, West Midlands supplier Craftmaster.

The painters were working to a very tight schedule, for the finished product would be unveiled to a world waiting with bated breath as soon as the top coat was dry…

Chapter 9

THE 50TH A1 UNVEILED

On Saturday 13 December 2008, more than 500 covenantors who had paid monthly instalments – many as little as the price of a pint of beer each week – proudly watched as the finished product was unveiled on the turntable in the National Railway Museum's Great Hall, which stands on the site of a former roundhouse that once housed A1s.

The completed A1 was formally unveiled at 1pm by a proud trust president Dorothy Mather. The event prompted another of frenzied media activity and priceless coverage in the national press and on TV. Those present watched in awe as a white sheet was pulled back to unveil the Pacific in all its glory.

Trust chairman Mark Allatt told the audience: "Today is another historic day for *Tornado*. All of the original Darlington-built Peppercorn class A1s were turned out in apple green livery and so it is entirely appropriate that *Tornado* should follow suit – just as Arthur Peppercorn's widow Dorothy first remembers them.

"Over the duration of its first boiler certificate, *Tornado* will carry all of the A1's historic liveries of LNER apple green with 'British Railways' on the tender, BR blue and BR Brunswick green, with both crest and emblem.

"*Tornado's* unveiling in apple green is the end of another chapter in the story of a project that many said could never be completed.

"In 1990 a group was formed with a vision and the determination to make it succeed – to build and operate a Peppercorn class A1 Pacific steam locomotive for main line and preserved railway use.

"Eighteen years later, and thanks to that shared vision and determination, *Tornado* turned its wheels in anger for the first time on 1 August 2008 in front of the world's press.

"It is thanks to our more than 2000 regular monthly and other donors, our sponsors led by William Cook Cast Products Limited and the hard work of our volunteers and contractors that the project has achieved so much."

Andrew Scott said: "Not only was York the final home of the Peppercorn class A1s but also the original drawings used to recreate this extinct class of steam locomotive are preserved in the NRM's archive centre Search Engine.

"Without the museum's involvement in hosting the locomotive during its main line trials and providing painting facilities, this fantastic project would not have been possible."

After the unveiling, *Tornado* went on public display inside the museum pending its inaugural trips, two York-Newcastle-upon-Tyne runs exclusively for covenantors and their guests over the weekend of 31 January/1 February. It was also agreed that No 60163 will go on display at the museum in between northern tours of duty.

Resplendent in BR apple green, A1 Pacific No 60163 Tornado stands inside the Great Hall in the National Railway Museum at York. MARK WALKER/A1SLT

INSET: The engine is publicly unveiled in its early BR livery for the first time. BRIAN SHARPE

Chapter 10

THE GREATEST MAIN LINE ADVENTURE BEGINS

Saturday 31 January 2009 marked a landmark moment in railway preservation. It was the occasion of the first public main line passenger-carrying run by *Tornado*.

A tidal wave of interest from the national media greeted what would be, as far as the general public was concerned, the true acid test.

It was also the day when it became fashionable again to like 'trains.' Back in the 50s, every schoolboy had at some stage been bitten by the 'steam bug'. It was par for the course with growing up, the main alternative pastimes being kicking a football around on the village green or collecting frogspawn in jamjars. Ian Allan built a publishing empire around his ABC Locospotters books, in which the numbers of each locomotive seen were underlined.

In retrospect, there was not much else to do in the days before rock and roll and football heroes conquered all. Indeed, to youngsters back in the days when steam still ruled the railways, locomotive crews were their idols: the ultimate ambition of every linesider was to 'cab' a main line express passenger locomotive.

Steam ended, to be replaced by preservation, in which die-hard enthusiasts sought to keep alive or rekindle the glories of the past. Sadly, for far too long everyone who admits to having a passion for anything running on flanged wheels has been the butt of regular 'jokes' from 'comedians', the press and TV.

However, it all changed on 31 January. Suddenly, everyone everywhere wanting to know, not knock.

Thanks to The A1 Trust, a new steam era had been born.

At York station, it was standing room only at best, as 2000 observers, many of them 'ordinary' families with toddlers, lined the platforms eager to glimpse history

Crowds lined the platforms at York on 31 January to glimpse Tornado backing on to its first main line public train. ROBIN JONES

Viewed from the tower of Durham Cathedral, Tornado heads 'The Peppercorn Pioneer' over Durham Viaduct en route for Newcastle on 31 January 2009 The Grade 2-listed viaduct, which comprises 11 semi-circular arches 60ft wide and is 76ft high, was completed in 1857. SJ TAYLOR/A1SLT

No 60163 crosses the King Edward Bridge over the River Tyne running back to Gateshead to turn after arrival at Newcastle on 31 January. DAVE HEWITT

The Angel of the North; Tornado arrives at Tyne Yard for servicing on 31 January. BRIAN SHARPE

Moment of truth: Tornado simmers in York station on 31 January waiting for the off. ROBIN JONES

The line of cars and photographers at Bridge 37 on the East Coast Main Line was typical of every vantage point between York and Newcastle on 31 January, and indeed, many other locations on the rail network for months to come, whenever Tornado is due to pass through. ROBIN JONES

LEFT: The A1 Trust operations director Graeme Bunker signs autographs after Tornado's faultless first passenger-carrying main line run. ROBIN JONES

RIGHT: Leaving the one-time Eastern Region at Shaftholme Junction and passing the North Eastern Railway's zero milepost, No 60163 Tornado gets into its stride at Joan Croft Junction on 1 February. BRIAN SHARPE

The new A1 arrives at Newcastle Central station with the 'The Peppercorn Pioneer' on 31 January. DAVE COLLIER

Tornado waits to depart from Newcastle Central with the return leg of its 31 January trip. ROBIN JONES

being made, or rather continued, as *Tornado* is not the first A1, or a replica, but the 50th member of the class.

Taking a serious photograph was barely possible: the best I could manage was a glimpse through safety glass of the magnificent apple green beast and its support coach backing from their National Railway Museum stable on to the Riviera Trains main line charter coaching stock, which had been brought into platform 10 by a modern Class 67 diesel.

Even then, I had to vie for space with teenage girls trying to capture the historic moment on mobile telephones, certainly an unlikely section of the transport history market. 'The Peppercorn Pioneer' was the inaugural trip for covenantors who had supported the project with monthly subscriptions and invited guests, a big thank you gesture to the people who had made it happen.

The A1 Trust had approached the Heritage Lottery Fund, a major benefactor to railway heritage in terms of the conservation of historic artefacts, on three occasions, only to be told it did not support new-build projects. An approach to the Millennium Commission also drew a blank, as The A1 Trust officials were told that the project was 'not unique enough'.

There are many who might well now disagree with the last statement. Accordingly, *Tornado* ended up being financed by its supporters and sponsors without the benefit of grant aid or other public funding.

The first trip appropriately ran to Newcastle-upon-Tyne and back, mirroring the final journey made by the last original A1, No 60145 *St Mungo*, on 31 December 1965.

Tornado's performance on its first trip turned out to be nothing special or startling. And that was the sheer beauty of it!

Passing Hadley Wood, Tornado heads 'The Talisman' southwards towards King's Cross on 7 February. GEOFF GRIFFITHS/A1SLT

The crowd fell silent as *Tornado* sounded its whistle and the first plumes of steam soared skyward, as it prepared to begin its journey at 12.07pm, hauling 13 carriages weighing a total of 550 tons behind it.

As No 60163 pulled out of York, under the control of driver Brian Grierson, traction inspector Jim Smith and fireman Steve Hanszar, history being made at every turn of its wheels, a huge cheer rose from the delighted masses.

Medicine for the miserable times of the credit crunch indeed, for here was a headline-grabbing British product, not only designed and built in Britain, but still owned by a British company (the Trust), unlike much else in these islands nowadays.

A brisk, outward run saw 'The Peppercorn Pioneer' reaching 60mph at Overton Grange, 70mph at Tollerton and 75mph just after Thirsk.

Its speed remained well over 70mph until it passed Durham.

Every one was according to schedule – and that made it so perfect.

As National Express chief executive Richard Bowker remarked: "The one thing about *Tornado* was the fact there were no signs of steam being emitted from areas where it was not supposed to."

Those travelling on the train savoured the dramatic views, sipping champagne. At every vantage point there was a platoon of photographers in attendance; at every road bridge a long line of cars parked along grass verges.

Many people simply brought their children out to wave at the shiny new locomotive and its train, as in days of yore.

It was as if the '15 Guinea Special' which had marked the end of BR steam on 11 August 1968 was being run again, only this time not to celebrate the end of a steam age, but the birth of a new one, for the 21st century.

A very conservative estimate gave the number of people who turned out in the freezing weather to view *Tornado* as 10,000.

At Newcastle, huge crowds, estimated at another 2000, were controlled by crush barriers and high-profile events patrols; while a Northumbrian pipe band greeted the arrival of the train.

Trust chairman Mark Allatt praised National Express officials not only for the way they organised the crowd control, but also for the fact that stewards crouched down behind the crush barriers to allow the public more photographic opportunities.

The return run, which began in Tyneside twilight, was less dramatic, with the train running on the slow line from Northallerton to York.

More crowds were there to greet the train, and by now the footplate crew had acquired celebrity status.

Operations director Graeme Bunker, who had also been on the footplate when *Tornado* made its first passenger-carrying run on the Great Central Railway last summer, was asked to sign a series of autographs, while radio journalists clamoured for a few words with anyone in the cab whose attention they could attract.

Needless to say, Mark was all but floating on air throughout the trip, as *Tornado* basked in unprecedented glory. *Tornado's* first main line passenger train is the end of another chapter in the story of a project that many said could never be completed.

"Many said the project would never get off the ground, and it did. Then they said the engine would never run.

"Finally, they told us we would never get permission to run it on the main line. Yet here we are.

"I believe that this is the future for steam on the main line. The time may come where it is no longer feasible to keep restoring the old locomotives to run over the national network, and new build will be the way ahead."

The second run of 'The Peppercorn Pioneer' came on the next day, Sunday 1 February.

The itinerary had been changed at the request of Network Rail and British Transport Police, so that there would not be large crowds gathering at Newcastle Central to see *Tornado* at the same time that a bumper gate was expected at the city's St James Park football ground for the local Premiership Derby game between Newcastle United and old enemies Sunderland.

A rearranged trip saw the train go from Doncaster, where local press coverage also enticed large crowds, to Durham. *Tornado* returned the train from there to York, with a modern diesel taking it back to Doncaster.

Tornado in full flight with the 21st century version of 'The Talisman' on Gamston Bank between Retford and Newark-on-Trent on 7 February. JASON CROSS

No 60163 at the exit of Gasworks Tunnel enters King's Cross station for the first time, heading 'The Talisman' on 7 February. GEOFF GRIFFITHS/A1SLT

Slightly disappointed but by no means dismayed, Mark said it was appropriate to run the train from Doncaster, because that was where the Peppercorn A1s were designed.

Also, 26 of the original A1s were built there in 1948/49, and the nascent A1 Trust had been based in Doncaster for a number of years before finding a permanent home in Darlington.

It was on Saturday 7 February that at last it was time for the ordinary fare-paying public to ride on the main line behind *Tornado,* which made a triumphant first entry into King's Cross, heading 'The Talisman' from Darlington, picking up at York, the train returning behind diesel traction. It was the Trust's first commercial main line trip. 'The Talisman' was British Railways' prestigious London-Edinburgh express, which symbolised the post-war renaissance of the East Coast Main Line. It was first run on 17 September 1956 – and regularly hauled by A1s.

At first, East Coast Main Line operator National Express, concerned at the

An A1's triumphant return to London: up to 2000 people packed into King's Cross to watch Tornado arrive from Darlington with 'The Talisman' on 7 February. GRAHAM NICHOLAS/A1SLT

anticipated number of sightseers wishing to see *Tornado* off from its Darlington birthplace at 7.45am, said spectators would not be allowed into the station because of fears that the platforms might be too slippy in the icy weather which had brought much of Britain to a standstill in the days beforehand.

The decision was widely criticised, and the company made a swift U-turn, prompting more expressions of gratitude from the trust. "We are all very grateful to National Express East Coast for making this a very special day for Darlington and *Tornado's* supporters," said Mark.

Meanwhile, south of Peterborough, route operator First Capital Connect agreed to open station platforms early so that crowds could watch No 60163 fly by on its first-ever visit to the capital.

Sadly, the run was marred by the irresponsible actions of several people who displayed a total lack of awareness of basic principles of railway safety and the appropriate trespass laws.

Delays caused by trespassers were compounded by the failure of an overhead line, resulting in a delay to the train in front, causing *Tornado* to lose its path.

Such delays echoed *Flying Scotsman's* East Coast Main Line comeback in the 1980s, when there were also several reports of trespassing.

'The Talisman' arrived at King's Cross half an hour late as a consequence of the problems en route.

Mark Allatt said: "At every stage we have warned people against trespassing on the lineside to see *Tornado*."

At King's Cross, it was estimated that up to 5000 people jostled to catch a glimpse of *Tornado* after it arrived and remained on display ffor a shorter period than had been planned, because of the delays.

The train was also a positioning move for charter train operator Steam Dreams' two Valentine's Day specials from London on 14 February, which both sold out within days, such was by now the appeal and standing of *Tornado* in the eyes of the public. Having worked the Up 'The Talisman' from York to King's Cross on 7 February, the 4-6-2 spent a week at Old Oak Common for 'fine tuning' to take place as part of its running-in programme. By that time, the A1 had covered less than 1000 miles since it first turned a wheel.

Prepared and given a fitness-to-run exam on 13 February, No 60163 was booked for a busy two-train duty 24 hours later when it hauled the morning Valentine's Day luncheon train and later, an evening diner.

The packed morning train was routed out of Waterloo down the South West Main Line to Basingstoke and Andover, then, turning left on the Laverstoke loop, returned via Southampton, Winchester and Woking.

The diner departed London Victoria for a 'Surrey Hills' trip via Staines, Byfleet, Woking and Guildford, returning via Redhill, East Croydon and Herne Hill.

Afterwards, *Tornado* and its support coach ran to the vast exchange goods depot at Hither Green on the Charing Cross-Tonbridge line in south-east London.

Given its fitness-to-run exam on the Sunday, *Tornado* departed for York the following morning, to await a very special duty indeed.

Tornado crosses Hurstborne viaduct in Hampshire with a Steam Dreams Valentine's Day special running from Waterloo to Eastleigh and back on 14 February. ED HURST

Chapter 11

THE NEW CROWN JEWEL OF STEAM!

Was it the finest hour for new-build Peppercorn A1 Pacific No 60163 *Tornado* – or the heritage railway movement overall? That was the question being asked on 19 February 2009 as The Prince of Wales and The Duchess of Cornwall officially named the £3-million locomotive at York station before it performed the rare honour of hauling the Royal Train to Leeds.

Watched by proud A1 Trust chairman Mark Allatt and the Duchess of Cornwall, Charles delivers his own tribute to Tornado and its builders. ROBIN JONES

At the head of the Royal Train, Tornado leaves York with a flourish of steam. DAVID F NEWBY

New A1 Pacific No 60163 Tornado heads the Royal Train back to York through Cross Gates. JEFF COLLEDGE

Prince Charles chats to the Tornado supporter on the platform. ROBIN JONES

Tornado heads through Micklefield while returning the empty Royal Train from Leeds to York. DAVE PEAKER/A1SLT

LEFT: While giving a speech extolling the virtues of steam, the prince was suddenly forced to use his script to waft away smoke from Tornado which had enveloped the podium. ROBIN JONES

Trust president Mrs Dorothy Mather at the naming ceremony at York station. ROBIN JONES

Royal steam train driver Bob Hart. ROBIN JONES

The prince unveils the nameplate. NEIL WHITAKER/A1 TRUST

Carrying the Prince of Wales' motif and the royal headcode, Tornado pulls away from York station. **ROBIN JONES**

Thousands of onlookers packed the platforms at York to catch a glimpse of the royal couple and *Tornado,* which backed onto the train around 9.30am after it had arrived behind a Class 67 diesel.

The prince was introduced to a host of local dignitaries and other supporters as an RAF band played. A1 Trust chairman Mark Allatt then introduced him to a selection of contractors, volunteers and locomotive builders.

Among the proudest on the platform to be introduced to the royal couple was Trust president and designer Arthur Peppercorn's widow – Dorothy Mather.

Charles praised the volunteers for all their dedication in producing *Tornado.* "Did you realise that the first A1 was built in 1948, the same year as I was born?" he asked. "A very good vintage, I promise you."

While he was delivering his speech in front of the locomotive on Platform 9, the prince was enveloped by clouds of smoke, causing him to halt and use his script to waft the vapour away as he gasped for air.

The prince said: "Nothing could give either myself or my wife greater pleasure than to be here at York station on this very special occasion of the naming of this new locomotive.

The nameplate and commemorative plaque unveiled by Prince Charles. ROBIN JONES

"I have nothing but the greatest admiration for the team of people who for the past 19 years, have been doing their utmost to produce this remarkable achievement."

He described *Tornado* as "a tribute to all of those incredible British engineering skills which made this country so famous."

He said: "The steam engine has been returned to the British main line and will again serve as an iconic and inspirational symbol of Britain."

Charles was presented with an OO scale model of *Tornado* in a glass case which had been specially commissioned by the trust from TMC, based at Hill Farm Holiday Cottages in Beck Hole, Whitby.

Chris Yates, owner of the company, said: "It is a big day for us all and very exciting for our work to be presented to the Prince of Wales.

Unveiling the nameplate, he named the A1 in honour of the crews of Britain's Tornado fighter jets in the first Gulf War. Two Hawk jets and a Tornado F3 then performed a flypast above the station.

Charles then donned a dust jacket and boarded the cab before the crew, including the Trust's operations director Graeme Bunker, showed him the controls.

Following a brief delay while *Tornado* was stoked, the A1 gave a loud whistle and pulled away for Leeds just after 10.40am, with driver Bob Hart at the regulator and Charles on the footplate as the band struck up again. The fireman was Frank Sutton and the traction inspector was Steve Chipperfield.

The royal couple later went on an impromptu walkabout in the centre of Leeds and other engagements in Yorkshire, while *Tornado* returned the train to York later in the afternoon.

The only other steam locomotive to have been given the honour of hauling the Royal Train on the national network, as opposed to preserved railways, in the heritage era is LMS Princess Coronation Pacific No 6233 *Duchess of Sutherland*.

Chapter 12

NOW IN REGULAR SERVICE

The royal naming completed, the 'firsts' for the 50th A1 were now coming fast and furious, and the crowds were getting bigger.

I t was calculated that the debut trip on 31 January saw 'The Peppercorn Pioneer' with its 13 coaches beat the pre-war timing for the much lighter 'Coronation'-named train by three-and-a-half minutes. The 74 minutes allowed for the 80¼-mile trip was possibly the fastest-ever steam schedule between York and Newcastle.

In its first venture across the Scottish border, Tornado heads the 'The Auld Reekie Express' over the Royal Border Bridge into Berwick-on-Tweed en route to Edinburgh Waverley on 28 February. Sadly, the man who founded tour operator Past-Time Rail, Bernard Staite, a driving force behind the campaign for steam to be allowed back on the national network in 1971, died on Good Friday, 10 April, following a long illness. Had it not been for his efforts, we may not now be seeing Tornado or any other steam locomotive on the UK main line. GEOFF GRIFFITHS/A1SLT

Tornado pulls into Edinburgh Waverley with the 'The Auld Reekie Express' on 28 February. PAUL CHANCELLOR

Classic East Coat Main Line panorama: Tornado leaves platform 2 at Edinburgh Waverley heading south for York on the return leg of the 'North Briton' railtour on 7 March. GORDON MCHATTIE

The legend grew from there, and with every trip that followed, more and more people, railway enthusiasts or not, wanted to know.

On Saturday 28 February 2009, *Tornado* made its first journey into Scotland with tour operator Past-Time Rail's 'The Auld Reekie Express' from York to Edinburgh.

It was *Tornado's* first trip with the new nameplates that had been unveiled by Prince Charles. A1 Trust operations director Graeme Bunker: "It was north of Newcastle when we really opened it out. We just walked away with it."

Tornado breasted the summit at Granthouse at a very commendable 66mph.

As expected, *Tornado* arrived in the Scottish capital to a storming reception. It brought memories of the four A1s shedded at Haymarket, which could be seen regularly at Waverley. Afterwards, No 60163 ran light engine over the Forth Bridge to spend the week at Thornton Junction, where preserved Gresley A4 4-6-2 No 60009 *Union of South Africa* is based.

A week later, on 7 March, No 60163 became the first A1 out of Edinburgh for 40 years with the 'North Briton' from Edinburgh to York.

Yet what most linesiders had desperately wanted to see more than anything was *Tornado's* first exit from the hallowed starting point of the East Coast Main Line.

The pinnacle of the preservation movement: Tornado runs along the clifftops near the Scottish border with Past-Time Rail's 'The Auld Reekie Express' on 28 February. Helen Pugh-Cook

One of three

Before Tornado entered service, B1 4-6-0 No 1306 and Class D49 4-4-0 No 246 Morayshire were the only two operational steam locomotives in Britain carrying LNER apple green livery.

The National Railway Museum's Gresley V2 2-6-2 No 4771 Green Arrow was withdrawn from traffic in spring 2008.

Apple green was also the last livery carried by A3 Flying Scotsman prior to its withdrawal in December 2005.

A first for King's Cross

The significance to enthusiasts and original project members of running in and out of the hallowed ground that is King's Cross was summed up by former A1 Trust chairman David Champion, when he rode on 'The Talisman' into the great London terminus on 7 February: "Many may remember how I used to say that giving people an A1 was like giving them back the Beatles?

Tornado storms through Doncaster with 'Yorkshire Pullman' on Saturday 18 April. GEOFF GRIFFITHS/A1SLT

Tornado on Tops

On 7 August 2008, Tornado was entered onto the TOPS (Total Operations Processing System), introduced in the 1960s primarily for the classification of diesel and electric locomotives.

Although Tornado's painted number is 60163, on the British main line Tornado has a designated TOPS number of 98863. The leading 98 describes a steam engine, the next 8 stems from the 8P power classification, and the final two numbers, 63, derive from the final two digits of 60163.

"Well, on the first run of No 60163 to King's Cross, as I leaned out of the carriage window coming out of Gasworks Tunnel, my jaw dropped as I saw all the platforms crammed with people wanting to witness this moment in history, and I thought to myself, 'You know, if I did have the Beatles on board, there couldn't be a bigger crowd to welcome us'."

However, the crowds had to wait until Saturday 18 April to see the first departure from King's Cross, when, hauling the luxury British Pullman stock for the first time, *Tornado* headed the 'Yorkshire Pullman' to York.

Tornado crosses Welwyn Viaduct, the notorious modern-day 'bottleneck' on the East Coast Main Line, with the 'Yorkshire Pullman' on 18 April. JAMES HAMILTON/A1SLT.

It was another momentous occasion, as it was the first time that a once familiar Peppercorn class A1 had departed from 'The Cross' in more than four decades.

The title 'Yorkshire Pullman' was first used on 30 September, 1935, and apart from the period of World War Two, survived for some years after end of steam. The original prestigious train started at Harrogate and was regularly hauled by *Tornado's* now extinct sisters south of Doncaster.

The train, on which dining-only seats cost £449 per head, consisted of 13 carriages, equating to about 550 tons, and ran at speeds up to 75mph. Champagne breakfast was served on the outward journey and a five-course meal on the way back to London. By Huntingdon, it was 15 minutes early, but lost time after being checked by a signal south of Peterborough.

A1 Trust chairman Mark Allatt enthused: "*Tornado's* first train from London's King's Cross station is the opening of a new chapter in the story of a project that many said could never be completed."

Director of engineering director David Elliott summed up these early tours: "In terms of performance, it's getting better with every trip we go out on. The engine is very nearly run in now and is therefore becoming a bit looser; but more significant is that the DB Schenker crews are becoming much more familiar with the engine.

"*Tornado* is not difficult to fire but it does need firing with a technique which is very specific to LNER Pacifics, and the DB Schenker crews handle a wide range of

Tornado streaks through Raskelf with the 'North Briton' to Edinburgh on 12 March. NEVILLE WELLINGS

What's in a Smokebox Plate?

Tornado's smokebox door carries the identification plate 51A, the code for Darlington Locomotive shed.

The cab side also carries the builders' plate, 'No 2195 Darlington 2008'.

locomotives and do not necessarily get that much experience on LNER types. But they are learning very fast and the steam raising is getting better and better all the time. We have been very pleased working with DB Schenker as their staff are very thorough in their procedures.

PEPPERCORN'S A1s: THE SPECIFICATIONS

Build dates	1948/49, 2008
Configuration	4-6-2
Leading wheel size	3ft 2in
Driver size	6ft 8in
Trailing wheel size	3ft 8in
Length	72ft 11.75in
Width	9ft 2.875in
Height	13ft 1in (Tornado 13ft)
Axle load	22.1 long tons
Weight on drivers	66.55 long tons
Locomotive weight	105.2 long tons
Tender weight	60.9 long tons
Locomotive and tender combined weight	166.1 long tons
Fuel type	Coal
Fuel capacity	9.0 long tons (Tornado 7½ tons)
Water capacity	5000gal (Tornado 6200gal)
Boiler	Diagram 118, 6ft 5in diameter, 29ft 2in length
Boiler pressure	250 psi
Cylinders	Three
Cylinder size	19in 26in
Fire grate area	50.0sq ft
Heating surface: tubes	1211.6sq ft
Heating surface: flues	1004.5sq ft
Heating surface: firebox	245.3sq ft
Superheater area	697.7sq ft
Valve gear	Walschaerts
Top speed	100mph
Tractive effort	37,397lb
Numbers	60114-60162, 60163

"We have had to fit spark arrestors to comply with current requirements and we have put a BR type self-cleaning smokebox arrangement in the front end of the engine, which does not seem to have affected the performance but works perfectly to the extent that we usually find only one dustpan of ash in the smokebox after each run.

"It has also been assessed on the East Coast Main Line for ride quality, and the hammer blow has been reduced.

"At 75mph, it complies with current group standards for ride and track force, including the new regulations about vibrations in locomotive cabs over a four-hour period."

Graeme Bunker added: "Without a doubt, *Tornado* is the most sophisticated steam engine operating in the UK today. For instance, in terms of the electrics alone, it has more on it than any other steam engine in the main line fleet.

"It is also running very economically too."

A support coach has been lined up for Tornado and is seen inside Darlington Locomotive Works. On its first main line trips, the A1 Trust has hired a support coach from another group to accommodate staff and equipment on trains.

Owned by a supporter of The A1 Steam Locomotive Trust, Mk1 brake corridor composite coach No S21249 was built at Swindon in 1961 to diagram 171, later seeing Department use before it became part of the Steam Locomotive Operators Association set in 1981. It went to Pullman Rail in 1984, the Lavender Line around 1989, and the Telford Steam Railway two years later. Arriving at the Great Central Railway (Nottingham) in July 2002, it was badly vandalised a year later, and rebuilt with parts from No 20134. It became operational again in May 2008, but needs further refurbishment and repainting before it could be used behind the A1. ROBIN JONES

Main line operator East Midlands Trains named a vehicle from its Class 222 Meridian unit 222003 Tornado in honour of the A1.

The dedication ceremony took place at Sheffield station and was carried out by Tim Shoveller, managing director of East Midlands Trains, and Andrew Cook, chairman of William Cook Cast Products, the A1 Trust's principal sponsor.

The vehicle concerned was also numbered 60163.

And the 'other' No 60163 drew up alongside on the platform opposite for good measure.

Tim Shoveller said: "When we found out that one of our Meridian trains shared a number with the first steam locomotive to be built for over 50 years, of course we wanted to mark that and naming this driving vehicle Tornado as well seemed appropriate.

"We're even more delighted to be able to do that in Sheffield. Sheffield is the home of the steel industry and many of the components of both our Meridian train Tornado and the steam engine Tornado were made by William Cook Cast Products.

"While our Meridians don't have the great romance and majesty of the steam locomotive, what we do have now are trains to London that are faster than ever."

Andrew Cook said: "William Cook has provided the driving wheels and all the other cast steel parts for this unique project. The company has also provided the substantial financial backing necessary to allow manufacture of the boiler and tender to take place."

No 60163 with the northbound 'Tyne Tornado' at Chapman's Bridge near Shipton on 12 March. GERALD NICHOLL

The 'Yorkshire Pullman' powers through Huntingdon at 75mph 15 minutes ahead of schedule BRIAN SHARPE

Seven chimneys, and five of them are steaming! Left to right are A4 No 60009 Union of South Africa, A2 No 60532 Blue Peter, A4 No 60007 Sir Nigel Gresley, A1 No 60163 Tornado and N7 0-6-2T No 69621. ROBIN JONES

Chapter 13

JOIN THE CLAN!

Ｎew, shiny, straight out of the box, like a Hornby Dublo locomotive fresh from unwrapping on Christmas Day. That was the view of many people who saw *Tornado* in its full BR apple green glory as it poised to haul its first revenue-earning passenger train.

It was a new experience for a large slice of the British population, who had never experienced the sight of a brand new steam locomotive appearing on the main line before. After all, it had been 49 years ago.

However, one of the last big tests of *Tornado* was – would it pass muster alongside the surviving LNER 'greats' of the likes of A4 streamlined Pacific No 60007 *Sir Nigel Gresley* and fellow Peppercorn product A2 4-6-2 No 60532 *Blue Peter*?

The cliché 'eagerly awaited' had for several months been banded about in relation to Barrow Hill Roundhouse's LNER II gala of 4-5 April 2009.

Barrow Hill has itself been one of the unique success stories of the latter-day preservation era, for it is the sole surviving rail-connected roundhouse in Britain.

A night shoot on 3 April saw Tornado, Blue Peter, Union of South Africa and Sir Nigel Gresley simmering in the yard. FRED KERR

Sir Nigel Gresley heads along the demonstration track with the Old Gentleman's Coach from the Keighley & Worth Valley Railway. ROBIN JONES

East Coast Main Line raw superpower spanning eight decades: Union of South Africa, Blue Peter, Sir Nigel Gresley, Tornado and, thrown in for good measure, N7 0-6-2T No 69621. ROBIN JONES

The LNER was by no means all about big glamorous Pacifics like A1s; N7 No 69621 is seen on a short demonstration goods train. ROBIN JONES

N7 0-6-2T No 69621 highlighting its Enfield Town heritage. ROBIN JONES

J17 0-6-0 No 65567, alongside O4 No 63601 and Butler Henderson. ROBIN JONES

Main road ahead: Tornado stands in the Barrow Hill yard waiting for its next assignment. ROBIN JONES

60163

RA 9

Romney, Hythe & Dymchurch Railway miniature Pacific Typhoon, built in 1926 by Davey Paxman, was renumbered 60164 – the next in sequence after Tornado – for its meeting with Britain's newest full-size steam locomotive. ROBIN JONES

Great Central Railway heavy freight O4 2-8-0 No 63601 is serviced inside the dimly lit roundhouse in the time-honoured way. ROBIN JONES

A roundhouse was a commonplace structure on railways across the world in the steam age. An engine shed was built around a turntable, each 'road' leading off the table providing a stable for a locomotive.

Dieselisation made them largely redundant, and their dim interiors illuminated by high Victorian windows were far from ideal for 'modern' traction.

Over the years since steam on the main line in 1968, many roundhouses were demolished. Some, like Camden roundhouse, were converted for other purposes, in that case an arts centre.

Local rock musician Mervyn Allcock was horrified at the thought of the former Midland Railway's Staveley roundhouse near Chesterfield being demolished, so he formed the Barrow Hill Engine Shed Society to save it.

In the late 90s, the society took over an empty Victorian building, and set out on a mission not only to preserve it, but also to make it pay.

Its rail connection having survived intact, under society ownership the site has become a depot for modern-day diesel locomotive operators. It is also the home of the Deltic Preservation Society, a group dedicated to the care of the English Electric behemoths that superseded the Pacifics on the East Coast Main Line.

Barrow Hill is therefore both a working site and a preservation venue.

It has also inaugurated a running line of its own for the hugely popular gala days and special events held each year, which features steam and modern traction or a combination of both.

Different themes are picked for the special events, many of them having absolutely nothing to do with the roundhouse's Midland heritage.

Historians have conjectured that the railway concept has its origins in the drama of ancient Greece, when someone had the idea of moving stage scenery quickly and effectively by mounting it on trolleys with wheels guided by grooves in the stage.

One of the greatest stages today as far as railway heritage is concerned, is Barrow Hill and its roundhouse.

Like any good stage, it can be quickly adapted to re-create any number of scenes from the steam age, whatever their geographical location – and the diesel and electric era too.

The grimy interior of steam sheds, with their high windows lighting the gloom and smoke hoods standing above filthy engines waiting to be cleaned, is nowhere better represented in the heritage sector.

Any period or region can be replicated, providing that you have the locomotives and stock. The Midland Railway roundhouse can so easily be adapted to suit another company's products, in this case those of the LNER.

Nothing here is airbrushed to perfection; the interior of the shed provides the public with a unique opportunity to experience the workaday setting of railways half a century and more ago – the times when short-trousered schoolboy trainspotters would sneak inside such buildings out of the watchful gaze of the shedmaster to glimpse the wondrous machines inside.

K1 2-6-0 62005 Lord of the Isles beneath the water tower at the roundhouse entrance. ROBIN JONES

The LNER II gala featured a unique line-up which could never have been staged in preservation before: *Tornado, Sir Nigel Gresley* and its sister A4 No 60009 *Union of South Africa,* plus *Blue Peter.*

Nobody would have thought when the last A1, No 60145 *St Mungo,* was withdrawn 43 years ago and scrapped after a failed preservation attempt, that such a sight would ever have been possible.

Tornado has been grabbing headlines for several months, but alongside its three LNER compatriots, it looked nothing special.

And that, on this occasion, was its overriding success; for it dovetailed in perfectly among these behemoths of the steam age, as if it had also been built 60 or more years ago.

For a casual observer unaware of its history, *Tornado* could have so easily been with us all that time.

Blue Peter, which has been stored at Barrow Hill while a decision is made about how best to return it to working order, was restored to LNER apple green livery specifically for this event to match *Tornado.*

The line-up understandably took centre stage, but the event saw one of the biggest gatherings of LNER engines in the heritage era.

A wealth of cameo scenes were being re-created inside the former Staveley Midland shed itself, courtesy of master of ceremonies extraordinaire Geoff Silcock, a widely respected, seasoned organiser of enthusiast photographic charters, who knows every trick in the book about how to bring the past spectacularly back to life.

Great Central Railway Robinson O4 2-8-0 No 63601 stood on a road alongside fellow GCR survivor Director 4-4-0 No 506 *Butler Henderson* and Great Eastern Railway J17 0-6-0 No 8217, both engines part of the National Collection.

Another main line visitor was LNER K1 2-6-0 No 62005 *Lord of the Isles.*

Outside, N7 0-6-2T No 69621 from the North Norfolk Railway mingled everywhere – occasionally becoming the Cinderella fifth locomotive in the glamour line-up outside, posing on the turntable with an Enfield Town plate across its smokebox or hauling a short rake of box and brake vans so typical of mid-1950s local trip services up and down the demonstration line.

Tornado at one stage lined up alongside yet another Pacific – in the form of *Typhoon* from the 15in gauge Romney, Hythe & Dymchurch Railway, long billed as the world's smallest public railway; while a miniature O4 greeted the full-size prototype.

One of the side attractions was the visiting teak North Eastern Railway directors' saloon, which starred as the Old Gentleman's Coach in the filming of *The Railway Children* on the Keighley & Worth Valley Railway. *Sir Nigel Gresley* took its turn to take the venerable vintage vehicle on short runs in the yard.

Tornado's pulling power saw more than 8000 people turn up over the two days of the gala – a record for the roundhouse.

Barrow Hill Engine Shed Society chairman Mervyn Allcock said: "It was easily our finest hour.

"The whole event was absolutely superb, but what made it really special was the line-up of A1, A2 and two A4s down the yard."

Chapter 14

DAVID ELLIOTT –
THE MAN WHO
MODERNISED THE A1

Our story of the development of East Coast Main Line Pacifics began with Nigel Gresley, the LNER Chief Mechanical Engineer who was succeeded by Edward Thompson, and in turn Arthur Peppercorn.

The legacy did not end there, because four decades later, the mantle was handed on yet again, to aircraft engineering expert David Elliott.

As we have heard, David offered his services when the A1 Trust was launched, and soon rose to the rank of director of engineering.

A modest and unassuming man, he declined the grandiose title of chief mechanical engineer held by his steam-era predecessors.

Instead, he prefers to think of himself as someone who would merely tweak a masterpiece of a design to make it conform to the railway legislation and demands of the 21st century.

In layman's terms, he is the one who has overseen the project on the technical side, and his modesty aside, the lion's share of the credit for its outstanding performances on the main line since its 31 January 2009 debut must be laid at his door.

David recalled: "It was almost ordained from the age of three that I would end up working on the railways.

"I had a very keen interest in railways from my very first train journey, and I was lucky enough to

A1 Trust director of engineering David Elliott: the man with the key both to Darlington Locomotive Works and to the future of British main line steam locomotive engineering. ROBIN JONES

David Elliott adjusting the wheel rotation motor on 23 October 2004. ROB MORLAND/A1SLT.

The name Tornado was chosen in honour of the RAF Tornado air crews that were flying at the time in the Gulf War – and ironically, the locomotive's engineering director had an air industry background! The honour of choosing the name was given to an early sponsor of the project. In January 1995, RAF officers of the Royal Air Force presented the Tornado nameplates to the trust during the frame-laying ceremony at Tyseley Locomotive Works in Birmingham. A1SLT

Inspecting the wheels of Tornado after it arrived at Loughborough on the Great Central Railway. BRIAN SHARPE

go through school doing A-levels in science subjects which resulted in a sponsored sandwich course with the London Midland Region at Derby starting in 1969. They sponsored me through a degree in mechanical engineering at Bradford University

I then went on through a series of career steps culminating in becoming traction maintenance engineer at Corkerhill depot in Glasgow for a year in 1976.

However, having reached the early stages of management on the railway, I looked upwards and didn't see a single job I wanted to do. So I moved out of that, and bar doing an MSC in air transport engineering, spent a total of 17 years in the aviation industry, working with helicopters, hovercraft and small six-winger aircraft.

"That culminated in me becoming commercial manager for Pilatus Britten-Norman, maker of the Islander, a 10-seater twin-engined aeroplane built for small islands which do not have runways capable of taking larger aircraft."

But once bitten by the railway bug…

"With privatisation, I started looking at getting back into railways again.

"By this time I'd done project management for some time so it seemed an obvious opportunity to follow.

"In 1996 I joined Adtranz Signal Ltd in Plymouth working on a Kuala Lumpur monorail project, for which the firm obtained the contract for the signalling part.

"However, the 1997 Far East financial crisis stopped the project and I spent the next two years tidying that up and doing other smaller projects."

Before that had sprung up a chance in a million, even though no remuneration was offered at the outset.

David recounted: "In 1991, I had expressed an interest in The A1 Steam Locomotive Trust and attended my first meeting in March 1991. It was the Trust's second meeting, the roadshow at the Great Northern Hotel at King's Cross.

"It was still very early days. As the first professional engineer who came along, I was very rapidly elevated to technical director – and I have been with the project ever since."

David had been an admirer of Peppercorn A1s since his boyhood, although he admits that he always regarded the A3s as the most graceful design because of the flowing curve of the running plate. He fondly recalled his first and only experience of an A1 in the steam age as it was entering its final phase.

"The 18 April 2009 trip with the 'Yorkshire Pullman' was a very nostalgic moment for me insofar as my one and only experience of an A1 dates from 1962.

"That was when my parents took my family on holiday from Kent up to the North East, where my father came from originally.

"On the way back my father wanted a bit more privacy so he upgraded us to first class on the 'Tees-Tyne Pullman' and booked the coupe compartment containing the family for the trip.

"When we arrived at King's Cross, I saw A1 No 60122 *Curlew* on the front. As an 11-year-old boy, I was deeply impressed with it. Because at a very early age I was interested in engineering, the A1 was fascinating to me even at the age of 11 or 12. As soon as we got home I got books out and read about these engines to see the developments that had gone on from Gresley's time."

By 2000, *Tornado's* frames had been moved to Darlington and many components had been assembled.

"It was apparent that it was necessary to have project engineering and management on site during the week when contractors were available to work on the engine. Previously we covered this at weekends using volunteers. The Trust offered me the opportunity to go part-time, working as director of engineering for the loco in Darlington."

David took the decision to move his family from Saltash in Cornwall, where they had chosen a house because it overlooked Isambard Kingdom Brunel's magnificent Royal Albert Bridge built in 1859 to carry the Cornwall Railway (later GWR) over the River Tamar to County Durham.

For the next four years, David worked six months of each year on the A1 as a contractor and the other six months on short-term contract work with Network Rail on a variety of modernisation projects.

When the Trust ordered the boiler in 2005, David was invited to go full-time until the locomotive was finished in December 2008.

"I am effectively the chief mechanical engineer," said David. "I was offered the title and I said 'this is a bit presumptious – I will accept it only when we own two locomotives'.

"I have been lucky being in a position to be able to effectively lay down engineering standards and sought out all the modifications.

"I have had very considerable help from experts within the industry and the movement. I am effectively the design authority for the engine."

But modesty aside, everyone out there is asking – is *Tornado* the finest steam locomotive of them all?"

David said: "In terms of what we have added to it, it is the most modern steam locomotive ever built.

"You will have endless arguments with the British Railways Standard brigade about the Britannia and *Duke of Gloucester*, which were later in design.

"I would contend that there weren't any better in terms of thermal efficiency, reliability and maintenance costs.

"This is because *Tornado* represents the end of 26 years of development from the first Gresley Pacific in 1922. The BR Standards were effectively new engines off the drawing board; where they got rid of a lot of problems, they introduced fresh ones.

"For example, in the early days, the wheels fell off the Britannias, which had to be withdrawn to have the axles sorted out. By contrast, there was no major modification made to the A1s between their introduction and their withdrawal."

David Elliott holds the certificate for the successful steam test, with boiler inspector John Glaze and A1 Trust officials on 11 Jan 2008. ROB MORLAND/A1SLT

David pointed to the in-depth testing which *Tornado* went through during its weeks on the Great Central Railway in summer 2008, including trial runs where it was matched against Britannia No 70013 *Oliver Cromwell*.

As well as standard tests; as technically a new design of locomotive, *Tornado* had to undergo specific extra tests to examine ride quality and track force, to assess the effect the locomotive would have on the main line track, as laid down by the Network Rail Safety Review Panel.

It was agreed in advance between the A1 Trust and the rail authorities that these could partially be done during its stint at Loughborough.

So on 25 September, *Tornado* ran through Kinchley curve at speeds of 10, 20, 30, 40, 50 and 60mph with a trailing saloon car fitted with monitoring equipment, including a Global Positioning System unit to measure the precise speed and distance travelled every yard.

Measurements were taken on board through 21 sensors attached to the locomotive, measuring pitch and roll, acceleration and deceleration, and also taken through the use of trackside sensors measuring side forces exerted on the track. These measurements were supplemented with freeze-frame footage of the position of the wheels as they passed.

The results were compared with control readings taken at the same site using No 70013 a fortnight later.

Trust officials were told that the preliminary results were described as producing 'no untoward signals'.

David said: "The Britannia ran through the same tests as ours went through, the argument being that even if we could not get enough data to give absolute values, we could say that *Tornado* was no worse than a Britannia.

"As it happened, our A1 was a lot better than the Britannia in terms of the loads it was putting into the track. The Britannias are not excessive, but ours was significantly better. This is borne out by the fact that if you are in the Britannia cab at speed, it is a fairly harsh gritty ride, whereas ours is smooth.

"At the end of the day, Chapelon in France achieved higher thermal efficiencies.

"The Americans in some respects achieved a much bigger maximum power output, but by UK standards, the fact that *Tornado* is a thermodynamically and mechanically advanced design, with roller bearings and a very good front end, is borne out by results.

"We have obtained a comparative study carried out by Darlington's engineering department on A1s and A2s in 1949, looking at their differences in hauling 'normal' 500-ton trains and heavy 600-ton trains.

"This produced a series of power versus speed, power versus cut off and other graphs for the A1s and A2s. In terms of efficiency there was little between them. The A1 consumed slightly more coal but slightly less water than the A2.

"This study was important for us because it gave us power speed curves for the locomotive.

"According to a timer who has travelled on our trains, we are bang on the 1949 curves with everything he had measured so far.

"So we have an engine that is not better or worse than the originals – but with the benefit that it had been put together with more care and love and is probably quieter and smoother."

Another question that automatically follows from laymen is – will *Tornado* ever break *Mallard's* world speed record.

The answer is no.

As already stated, at the time of writing, paperwork is being completed with a view to having *Tornado's* builders fulfil their dream of seeing it run at 90mph on the main line – making it the only steam locomotive in Britain permitted to do so, and the second fastest in the world after Deutsche Reichsbahn Pacific No 18.201, which is permitted to run in Germany up to 110mph.

Regular 90mph steam operation was last seen in Britain in 1967 with the Bulleid Merchant Navy Pacific locomotives operating on the Waterloo to Bournemouth line.

David said: "There is a question as to whether we should do a 10 per cent overspeed – and we hope one day we will get the opportunity to do a magic ton.

"But we could never go as far as *Mallard*. Tests on *Mallard* at 125mph showed that more than 400hp was saved because of the streamlining.

"The A1 has divided drive and I am not convinced that at that speed it would not be likely to suffer damage. The A1s were not designed for high speeds, but to roll along at 75mph with loads of 500-600 tons and that is impressive in itself."

However, Deutsche Bahn had informed the Trust that if it ever visited Germany, *Tornado* would be allowed to run 'as fast as they like'.

So will *Tornado* ever go abroad?

"We have briefly discussed the possibility, and would like to take *Tornado* to Meiningen Works as a thank you for them building the boiler," said David.

"If a suitable offer came up which did not prejudice any opportunities for running in the UK, and funded the cost of doing it, we would consider going to Europe.

"If we did a tour through France and Germany to Austria and back, for instance, it would pay in terms of filling trains, but there would be the cost of having to fit European safety systems.

"At the moment, we can occupy every hour that *Tornado* is capable of operating in Britain and that is not likely to diminish next year. Those who have had it, like the Great Central Railway and Barrow Hill, are pleading for us to take it back. Where we go, crowds follow.

"To me, the staggering thing is just how well it has worked out of the box."

Chapter 15

EQUALLING 'THE ELIZABETHAN'…

with a little help from BBC *Top Gear*

T*ornado* quickly proved its worth as a magnificent performer on the East Coast Main Line. But was it a 'great' locomotive, in the mould of *Flying Scotsman* and *Mallard,* able to rub shoulders with the LNER's finest?

The historic test came on Saturday 25 April 2009, when No 60163 was involved in a 21st-century Race to the North, from King's Cross to Scotland.

Not constrained by the steam era permanent speed restriction of 20mph, A1 Pacific No 60163 Tornado heads the 25 April 2009 King's Cross-Edinburgh 'The Cathedrals Express' through Peterborough on the centre road. BRIAN SHARPE

The event would evoke memories of the great age of British steam, back in the 30s when the LMS and LNER were locked in a constant promotional battle in order to be able to claim the fastest train services from Euston and King's Cross to Scotland.

However, it was not a case of two Big Four companies seeing who could get there in the shortest time – but an A1 taking on the A1! In the weeks leading up to the run, talks had taken place between the A1 Trust and the BBC, producer of the BAFTA, multi-NTA and International Emmy Award-winning TV motoring show *Top Gear*.

The idea was for *Tornado* to 'race' a car and a motorcycle from the late 1940s from King's Cross to the Scottish capital. With an estimated 350 million viewers worldwide from the United States to Australia, *Top Gear* would showcase *Tornado* to an unprecedented audience as far as the steam world was concerned.

A somewhat blackened Jeremy Clarkson interviewed on film outside Edinburgh Waverley after eight gruelling hours on the footplate of Tornado. JONATHON GOURLAY

There would be no breaking of the speed limit on either roads or railways. The A1 would, of course, be held up by water stops, while the car and motorcycle would

The Jaguar XK120 used in the Top Gear challenge following its arrival at Edinburgh's Balmoral Hotel. JONATHON GOURLAY

The Vincent Black Shadow motorcycle – a superb machine indeed, but two wheels were never going to compete against a brand new 4-6-2 in full flight! JONATHON GOURLAY

Race to the north: £3-million new-build Peppercorn A1 Pacific No 60163 Tornado powers through Cromwell north of Newark-on-Trent with the 25 April 'Cathedrals Express' from King's Cross to Edinburgh with Top Gear presenter Jeremy Clarkson on the footplate. BRIAN SHARPE

be delayed by traffic lights in and out of London, and any other hold-up. Furthermore, they were to be restricted to using the Great North Road of the late 40s – the A1.

The BBC insisted on utmost secrecy for the trip, one reason being given was fears for safety if paparazzi tried to film any of the road contestants by overtaking them on the A1 and the public tried to follow suit. Steam Dreams, the railtour operator run by the Trust's operations director Graeme Bunker, organised the trip, with Network Rail, crew provider DB Schenker and coach supplier Riviera Trains giving their services at cost price.

Steam Dreams marketed the outing as one of its 'Cathedrals Express' day trips, which offer walk-on steam journeys from London normally to cathedral cities. Around 200 regular Steam Dreams customers were personally telephoned and asked if they were prepared to pay £250 to go on a trip from King's Cross to Edinburgh. All that the passengers were told in advance was that the special would be 'an attempt to achieve the fastest steam hauled trip between the two cities since the 1960s'. There was no mention of *Top Gear*.

So *Tornado* (of late 40s design), heading the Riviera Trains 'Royal Scot' carmine and cream set of nine coaches offering full dining facilities (plus maroon support coach), was pitched against a 1949 Jaguar XK120 sports car and a 1949 Vincent Black Shadow motorcycle. *Tornado* had Edinburgh's Waverley station as the finishing point for the 392-mile jaunt, while its competitors had to reach the city's Balmoral Hotel.

Despite the secrecy, word of the trip spread like wildlife along the enthusiast 'grapevine' – in the 21st century aided and abetted by fervent postings on internet

On the way back: Tornado crosses the King Edward bridge across the River Tyne on 26 April, en route to Tyne Yard with the empty stock. Extra scenes were filmed with Jeremy Clarkson on the footplate with this empty stock working. DAVE HEWITT

discussion groups and backed up by mobile telephones – and many vantage points along the route ended up with their fair share of photographers. Hundreds if not thousands turned up at the lineside to watch the train speed past.

The competitors were scheduled to set off from King's Cross at 7.25am, but *Tornado* left about 90 seconds late. No special path was created for the one-way steam train but the timings were planned to avoid clashes with public services. A helicopter could be seen flying above the East Coast Main Line to film the train, which gained 15 minutes en route to Grantham, as it was diverted on to the fast line up Stoke Bank, having been booked for the slow line. Ironically, the special, which ran as 1Z63, was forced to reduce speed approaching Waverley station by a local 'stopper' running in front.

Nevertheless, *Tornado* arrived a minute early at 3.26pm, having taken exactly eight hours – and if you take off the four water stops at Grantham, York (where No 60163 received a fresh crew), Newcastle (Tyne Yard including coal) and Berwick, that brought the timing down to a extremely commendable 'steam age' six-and-a-half hours. So a preservation era record timing for the run was claimed. Surprisingly, Jeremy Clarkson, core presenter of the *Top Gear* programme and well known for driving long distances to test impossibly expensive new cars, did not as expected take the wheel of the XK120.

The three Top Gear presenters, Richard Hammond, James May and Jeremy Clarkson, compare notes outside the Balmoral Hotel after arrival in Edinburgh. JONATHON GOURLAY

Instead, he travelled on the footplate of No 60163 throughout, handling the fireman's shovel on occasions; his face blackened with soot by the time the train reached Edinburgh. The Jaguar was driven by colleague James May; and the Black Shadow ridden by Richard 'Hamster' Hammond, the man who survived a well-documented rocket-powered car crash two years ago.

A1 Trust director of engineering David Elliott said: "We understand we set a new preservation era record for steam between King's Cross, Peterborough, Grantham and York.

"Some of that was down to us taking only 15 minutes for a water stop at Grantham instead of the booked 21.

"What was impressive was that *Tornado* strode on at 75mph for long distances."

A1 Trust chairman Mark Allatt said: "The timings we achieved for the run, minus of course the water stops, were the same as those on 'The Elizabethan'."

That is certainly an accolade of the highest magnitude. With the onset of World War Two, express passenger services and races to the north took a back seat as the LNER prioritised the movement of troop trains along the East Coast Main Line. As Britain began to pull out of the years of austerity, some of the glamour services returned. It was in 1949 that British Railways launched its 'Capitals Limited' non-stop service from King's Cross to Edinburgh, in a bid to regain some of the lost prestige of pre-war steam. It completed the journey in six hours 30 minutes.

Following the accession to the throne of Queen Elizabeth II, the name was changed to reflect the new Elizabethan age that was unfolding. The inaugural run of the rebranded train came on 29 June 1953, with A4 Pacific No 60028 *Walter K Whigham* in charge.

'The Elizabethan' was always hauled by one of the A4s fitted with a corridor tender so that crews could be changed while on the move. No A1s were used: they did not have corridor tenders, because they were equipped only with steam braking, whereas the Gresley engines had the necessary vacuum braking and the tender couldn't be exchanged.

In 1954, British Transport Films produced a 20-minute film about 'The Elizabethan' featuring A4 No 60017 *The Silver Fox*. Titled *'Elizabethan Express'*, it has been described as best film documentary about the operation of a steam-hauled express ever made. It was directed by Tony Thompson, with a poetic commentary written by Paul Le Saux and music by Clifton Parker, who later wrote the music for the 1959 version of *The Thirty-Nine Steps,* which also featured an A4.

However, despite its high profile, 'The Elizabethan' was in reality steam's last fling on the East Coast route. Record holder No 60022 *Mallard* was the last steam locomotive to haul the Down non-stop 'Elizabethan', on 9 September 1961. Deltics took over. The inaugural diesel-hauled 'The Elizabethan' departed King's Cross on Monday 18 June 1962 behind D9012 *Crepello* – but it was not the same.

The new service involved a stop at Newcastle to allow crew changes: it was said that London crews were prepared to travel in the comparatively cramped Deltic cab for the duration of the 393 miles, but those from Edinburgh's Haymarket shed were not.

The 1962 winter timetable, which came into force from 10 September, saw the final withdrawal of 'The Elizabethan', which was downgraded into a King's Cross-Newcastle train. Graeme Bunker said that the cost of the trip was covered by the fare-paying passengers – and all it cost the BBC (and in turn licence fee payers for that matter) was a token appearance fee.

Better still, because the track access, locomotive crew and coach rake were provided at cost price, a profit was made for the A1 Trust, which by this stage was trying to eat its way into £800,000 worth of debts incurred in finishing *Tornado*. Additionally, National Express East Coast helped ticketing and provided discounted tickets for the participants' return journeys to King's Cross. So how did the race pan out?

Understandably, the BBC was keeping the details of the winner close to its chest, as well as the date for the transmission of the programme featuring *Tornado,* although it was soon well known that the bike came third. As expected, pundits had been hard at it, some reckoning that *Tornado* made the better time, others believing that the car arrived first.

Indeed, the car had the advantage of the 'new' A1 in places, where it has been upgraded into a motorway or dual carriageway, and did not have to follow the original A1 into now-bypassed towns and villages, the route that existed in the 1940s.

"It would have been impossible to attempt a true historical re-creation," said Graeme. "If we had done so, we would not have needed so many water stops.

"It was done just for fun and entertainment."

As is usual in the case of BBC TV productions, no firm date is forecast for the programme's on air transmission, but late June has been suggested.

Following the race, the 4-6-2 moved light engine and support coach to Grosmont on the North Yorkshire Moors Railway on Monday 27 April for a 10-day gala stint, during which time it would haul a rake of LNER Gresley teak coaches for the first time.

Incidentally, the *Top Gear* programme was not the first time by any means that *Tornado* had been the star of a TV show. In addition to numerous appearances on news bulletins, for years a BBC crew had filmed the project at certain points on the journey, up to and including arrival and operation of *Tornado* running at the Great Central Railway.

The resulting film was used to make a 30-minute documentary film, *Absolutely Chuffed: The Men Who Built A Steam Engine,* first broadcast on BBC 4 on 16 October 2008, as part of its Golden Age of Steam season. *Tornado* and The *Tornado* project was also partly featured in the BBC4 documentary episode *The Last Days Of Steam,* in series 8 of the Time Shift documentaries, on Channel 5's *How Do They Do It?* and in BBC2's magazine programme *Working Lunch* broadcast on 3 December 2007.

Chapter 16

AN A1 HAULING GRESLEY TEAKS

O ne of the biggest success stories has been the North Yorkshire Moors Railway, which has established itself as Britain's most popular heritage line with more than 300,000 passengers each year.

The heritage line runs from Pickering to Grosmont, the junction with Network Rail's Esk Valley branch from Middlesbrough to Whitby via Battersby. However, in recent years, the NYMR has extended passenger services from Grosmont into Whitby with resounding success.

The route is part of the Whitby & Pickering Railway planned in 1831 by rocket builder George Stephenson as a way of opening up the hinterland of the port of Whitby. Opened in 1836, it was originally worked by horse-drawn carriages, taking two and a half hours to travel from Whitby to Pickering before it was acquired in 1845 by the York & North Midland Railway, which re-engineered it so it could accept steam locomotives.

In 1854, the route became part of the North Eastern Railway, absorbed into the LNER in 1923. It was one of the many country routes earmarked for closure by Dr Richard Beeching in his report of 1963, and the last trains ran in 1965.

However, in 1967, the North Yorkshire Moors Railway Preservation Society was formed, and began running heritage services over part of the route in 1973.

Eventually, the railway was relaid as far south as Pickering, the headquarters of the line.

Its success has been largely due to a combination of stunning moorland scenery and its use for location filming in the TV 60s police drama series *Heartbeat*.

Much of the rolling stock reflects the line's heritage. It is the home of A4 Pacific No 60007 Sir Nigel Gresley and also the LNER Coach Association, which restores Gresley teak coaches for use on the line. From 1-10 May 2009, the railway organised a special spring steam gala – with none other than *Tornado* topping the bill.

For LNER aficionados, it was a dream come true: the chance to see an A1 in

As it would have looked in 1948: hauling Gresley teak stock, Tornado rounds the curve at Darnholm with the 9.30am from Grosmont on the North Yorkshire Moors Railway on 2 May 2009. BRIAN SHARPE

apple green livery hauling a rake of Gresley teak coaches once more. However, the historic appearance of No 60163 was hampered at the outset by a slight hiccup. For it was twice stopped for emergency repairs.

A leak in a fusible plug meant that *Tornado,* which had arrived on the heritage line via the Esk Valley branch on the afternoon of Monday 27 April light engine from Newcastle following the *Top Gear* trip, and underwent gauging trials the next day, missed a press trip on Thursday 30 April while repairs were carried out at Grosmont shed.

Tornado made its NYMR debut on Friday 1 May and ran for the next two days, as bumper crowds turned out to see it.

However, the problem did not go away, and on the Saturday evening, the locomotive was taken out of service and hauled back to Grosmont by the National Railway Museum's Class 37 diesel D6700, which was on loan to the line.

The railway's management stressed that the lug had not failed, but the locomotive was stopped because of the leak purely as a precautionary measure. Grosmont shed had most of the spares needed to make a permanent repair – but not all.

A frantic call to the Great Central Railway, where *Tornado* had undertaken its test runs, led to that line's engineer Craig Stinchcombe and his team turning out at 7am on the Sunday to make two new fusible plugs from blanks held in store at Loughborough shed.

The Great Central team were hailed as heroes for their rapid response, and the new plugs were delivered to the NYMR later that morning. After the faulty plug was

Tornado leaving Goathland
with its matching rake of
teak carriages on 2 May.
BRIAN SHARPE

replaced, *Tornado* completed a successful light engine run to Goathland in the evening and returned to traffic on the Monday.

A1 Trust operations director Graeme Bunker said: "We identified and dealt with the problem very quickly. We realised that we needed some spares that were not available at Grosmont.

"The Great Central really helped us out by making the fusible plugs at short notice."

For the rest of the gala, *Tornado* performed faultlessly and again proved a massive draw, as 13,100 people travelled on the trains, producing bumper receipts of £170,000 despite the credit crunch. On the Sunday, both it and No 60007 headed passenger trips along the Esk Valley line from Grosmont to Batterby and back. One of the trips effectively formed a Battersby-Pickering through service.

A delighted NYMR general manager Philip Benham said: "By far the biggest factor for this huge attendance was *Tornado*, although many people came to see Sir Nigel Gresley too."

Afterwards, *Tornado* returned to main line duties, hauling the first leg (King's Cross to York) of Steam Dreams' three-day 'The Coronation' trip from London to Edinburgh and Dundee on Saturday 16 May, and the York to King's Cross final leg on Monday 18 May.

The following Saturday, *Tornado* was booked to haul the outward leg to Steam Dreams' trip from King's Cross to York, where it will go on display at the National Railway Museum between northern duties.

On Saturday 30 May, *Tornado* was booked to haul sections of two of Pathfinder Tours' 'Severn Coast Express' trips, the first taking the train from Gloucester through Chepstow and Newport to Cardiff, return journey through the Severn Tunnel to Bristol Temple Meads. The second trip would see *Tornado* haul the train Bristol Temple Meads to Taunton and then along the West Somerset Railway to Minehead.

That was arranged as a positioning move to allow No 60163 to spend 31 May-17 June in service on what is Britain's longest standard gauge heritage railway. It was due to star in the 12-14 June mixed traffic weekend, working trains alongside a fleet of 1960s diesels.

Furthermore, the LNER-design locomotive was booked to link up with another of the 'Big Four' company's steam fleet during its stay. The Waverley, the last paddle steamer built for the LNER, was due to run from Penarth pier near Cardiff on both 8 June and 12 June to Minehead, connecting to trains hauled by *Tornado*.

Waverley was ordered by the LNER in 1946 to replace a paddle steamer of the same name sunk at the Dunkirk evacuation. *Tornado* was booked to return to its 'first' birthplace, Tyseley Locomotive Works, for an open weekend on 27-28 June, to meet up with another locomotive that made Darlington famous nearly two centuries before – Beamish Museum's working replica of Stockton & Darlington Railway pioneer *Locomotion No 1*.

The A1s were built before British Railways introduced its Mk1 coaching stock in 1950. Tornado is seen hauling a rake of maroon Mk1s past Abbot House south of Goathland during its successful visit to the North Yorkshire Moors Railway. DAVE RODGERS

During the summer of 2009, *Tornado* is scheduled to work Past-Time Rail's successful 'Torbay Express' from Bristol to Paignton and on to Kingswear along another heritage line, the Paignton & Dartmouth Steam Railway.

Much attention was focused on its Past-Time 'Golden Hind' trip from Bristol to Plymouth and return on Saturday 11 July, taking in the notorious South Devon banks.

'The Waverley', *Tornado*'s 3-4 October debut over the spectacular Settle to Carlisle line, a trip promoted by the A1 Trust, quickly sold out.

From 24 October to 7 November, *Tornado* has been booked to run on the Severn Valley Railway, Britain's second most popular heritage line in terms of passenger numbers.

Each day, more requests to hire *Tornado* are received by the A1 Trust, and bookings continue to soar. For it is clear that the A1 has captured the 21st century public imagination like no other railway locomotive. Its sparkling performances and resounding success stand as a testament to the faith and determination of the visionaries who launched the project in 1990 and those who laboured relentlessly to make an impossible dream come true.

Chapter 17

AN A1 FOR ALL SEASONS

During the building of *Tornado,* the question of the livery in which it would appear took a back seat. When pressed, A1 Trust officials would merely say, quite correctly as it turned out, that it would first run in 'undercoat'. However, as assembly became well advanced, there was only one choice, at least for the locomotive's debut and first few years in traffic.

It had to be the same livery as the original A1s had been outshopped in… LNER apple green, but with BRITISH RAILWAYS in large capital letters on each side of the tender, instead of the initials of the 'Big Four' company.

Brand-new A1 Pacific No 60129 in lined blue livery stands outside Doncaster 'Plant' in June 1949. The engine has a rimless chimney and the front numberplate in the higher position and would later be named Guy Mannering. COLOUR-RAIL

The A1s appeared after nationalisation, but before British Railways had decided on a corporate livery for its locomotives. Accordingly, the pre-war LNER livery was simply modified, and the first 30 A1s were turned out in it.

Soon, a radical new colour scheme for express passenger locomotives was selected – lined blue. Other passenger locomotives were to adopt Great Western Railway-style Brunswick green, while mixed traffic locomotives were to appear in London & North Western Railway lined black.

The final 19 A1s appeared in the blue livery, and all but one of the rest were repainted into the colour scheme when they came up for overhaul.

However, British Railways soon had second thoughts about the express passenger blue livery, as it faded badly. Around 1951, it was replaced with lined Brunswick green.

There were two variations of the latter colour scheme. The first (1948-65) appeared with the 'lion and wheel' logo, showing a lion standing over a spoked wheel on which the words British Railways were displayed. The second logo (1956-65) featured a lion holding a wheel sitting in a crown, with the words British and Railways to left and right.

The A1s carried both these schemes. It is intended that *Tornado* will appear in all four colour schemes during its 10-year boiler ticket, ringing the changes and generating yet more publicity for this locomotive, which undoubtedly is equally magnificent in any livery.

How Tornado will look in future years: Tornado in British Railways-lined Brunswick green with emblem on tender. This is a computer-manipulated view of No 60163, then still in works grey, arriving at Leicester North with a passenger service during the Great Central Railway's 10-12 October autumn steam gala. JASON CROSS

Chapter 18

NEW BUILD –
THE FUTURE OF
BRITISH STEAM?

The resounding success of *Tornado* has highlighted what many believe is the future of railway preservation – new build. As we have seen, No 60163 was not the first new locomotive to be built by the heritage railway movement, and it certainly will not be the last.

Indeed, in the same year that the 50th A1 turned a wheel for the first time, a replica representing a locomotive of far greater historical importance was unveiled to the public.

BR Standard Pacific No 72008 Clan MacLeod
at Crewe North. NEVILLE STEAD/SSLT

British Railways Standard 3MT 2-6-2T No 82000. A new example of the class is being built at the Severn Valley Railway. BRITISH RAILWAYS

The replica of Trevithick's Catch-Me-Who-Can at Barrow Hill roundhouse in August 2008. ROBIN JONES

In 1808, the inventor of the railway locomotive, Cornish engineering giant Richard Trevithick, demonstrated his Catch-Me-Who-Can on a circle of track near the site of the future Euston station. Built at Hazeldine Foundry in Bridgnorth, Shropshire, by engineer John Urpeth Rastrick, the locomotive hauled a single carriage, and the pair therefore comprised the world's first steam passenger train.

A working standard gauge replica has been built in Bridgnorth at the Severn Valley Railway workshops by the local Trevithick 200 group to mark the bicentenary of the event. Comprising very basic but nonetheless efficient steam technology, it cost around £50,000 to build – a tiny fraction of the cost of *Tornado*!

For years before *Tornado* was finished, A1 Trust officials and covenantors were asking themselves the question – what next, if anything?

The all-new 900mm gauge 2-8-2 tank engine built at Dampflokwerk Meiningen, which supplied the boiler for Tornado. DAMPFLOKWERK MEININGEN

The smokebox for the new Clan, Hengist, at the South Devon Railway in 2009. ROBIN JONES

The original GWR 4-6-0 No 1014 County of Glamorgan inside Swindon Works on 13 May 1962. GWS

Willington Hall is unloaded at the Llangollen Railway on 4 November 2005, ready for dismantling its boiler to become the key part of a new GWR Grange, while the frames and cylinders will be used to build a new GWR County. 6880 BETTON GRANGE PROJECT

Broad gauge replica Firefly and coach at Didcot Railway Centre. ROBIN JONES

The firebox and boiler for the new G5 0-4-4T at Great Northern Steam in Darlington. ROBIN JONES

Original London Brighton & South Coast Railway buffers fitted to the front beam of the Bluebell Railway-based replica of Brighton Atlantic No 32424 Beachy Head. BLUEBELL RAILWAY

At the time of writing, around £700,000 needs to be raised to repay the debts incurred in completing the A1; and while fundraising continues in earnest, the Trust is giving much serious thought to this question.

Eventually, he said, the question will be asked – should we build another?

Many A1 Trust supporters have long favoured the building of a replica of Gresley P2 Mikado *Cock o' The North*, a glaring omission from Britain's heritage fleet. There are few today who remember seeing the original, but it has such a distinctive appearance that to the general public it would be at least every bit as eye-catching as *Tornado*.

This would be the choice of director of engineering David Elliott, who offered his personal opinion: "The 'P2' is sex on wheels – it is drop-dead gorgeous. There is also around 65 per cent commonality of parts with the A1, so we have many of the patterns already made."

Indeed, with the National Railway Museum having in May 2009 unveiled its restreamlined LMS Princess Coronation Pacific No 6229 *Duchess of Hamilton* in its as-built 1938 condition, for static display at York in the first instance, would it not be marvellous to be able to produce a line-up of the most powerful locomotives of the two great rivals in the north to reflect the steam zenith that was the 30s?

There are now several standard gauge new-build projects ongoing in Britain, some at an advanced stage. However, few if any have been able to emulate the giant of the fundraising machine of The A1 Trust, let alone its marketing and PR campaign, prime ingredients behind the success of the *Tornado* project.

In 1997, the Standard Steam Locomotive Company (http://72010-hengist.org) was formed, also to recreate an extinct type of Pacific for the main line, in this case the British Railways Standard Class 6 mixed traffic engine, otherwise known as 'Clans'.

Ten of them were built as part of the 1951 Locomotive Renewal Programme, numbered 72000-9, and all were allocated to the Scottish Region where they were named after Scottish Clans.

A national steel shortage in 1954 and the Modernisation Plan the following year ended plans to build another 108. While they found favour with Scottish crews, they were criticised in other areas, and the last was withdrawn in 1966.

A locomotive which comparatively few enthusiasts had seen or remembered was a brave choice indeed for a new-build project which would depend on mass public support, but nonetheless was laudable in view of plugging another gap.

The new locomotive will be the one that would have been the next in line, No 72010 *Hengist*. Steady progress has been made by the group in assembling parts, the biggest of which completed to date being the frames, which were due to have the cab and smokebox fixed to them at engineer Ian Riley's Bury workshop in 2009. However, far more needs to be done on the fundraising front to finance major components like the boiler, wheels and cylinders.

GWR Grange 4-6-0 No 6856 Stowe Grange inside St Philips Marsh shed at Bristol on 27 July 1963. TB OWEN/6880 PROJECT

Following in the footsteps of Tornado: the driving wheels for the new GWR 4-6-0 No 1014 County of Glamorgan were cast by A1 Trust principal sponsor William Cook at its Sheffield plant early in 2007. WILIAM COOK

One of the most recent major new-build projects to be launched, one which has already made significant inroads into fundraising for the initial stages, is a Llangollen Railway-based scheme to build a new LMS unrebuilt Patriot 4-6-0, none of which survived into preservation.

The LMS-Patriot Project (www.lms-patriot.org.uk) has announced that the locomotive will be numbered 45551, what would have been the next in sequence of the Patriots under British Railways, and it will be named *The Unknown Warrior* and serve as a permanent memorial to all those who fought and died in World War One and all subsequent wars.

Tyseley Locomotive Works (www.vintagetrains.co.uk) has for several years been building a replica of a LNWR 'Bloomer' 2-2-2, although there are no plans to take it on the main line.

In 2008, the North British Locomotive Company (www.nbloco.net) announced a scheme to build not one but two of Gresley's extinct B17 4-6-0 Sandringham class, one being an example of the 'Footballer' derivatives named after Football League clubs. The idea is that one will run on the main line and visit heritage railways, while the other will remain on static display. Parts will be interchangeable so one of them will always be operational. So far, an original tender has been obtained and a cab built. However, not all new-build projects need be anywhere near as expensive as *Tornado*, provided that they use second-hand components.

Ten of the final rusting hulks from Barry scrapyard were bought by the local council for an abortive scheme to build a national railway museum for Wales in Cardiff. Eventually, the locomotives were released for use in other preservation projects.

One of them, Western Region Hall 4-6-0 No 7927 *Willington Hall*, was taken to Llangollen for the boiler to be donated to a project to build a new Great Western Railway Grange 4-6-0, to be known as No 6880 *Betton Grange*.

The frames and cylinders of *Willington Hall* were then taken to Didcot Railway Centre for use in a Great Western Society (www.didcotrailwaycentre.org.uk) project to re-create Hawksworth County No 1014 *County of Glamorgan*, recalling the location of Barry scrapyard which made the project possible.

The dismemberment of one GWR locomotive and its reassembly into two others is possible because of the Swindon empire's insistence of standardised parts which would be interchanged between several locomotive types.

Special mention must be made of the Grange project, which has held two hugely successful galas at Llangollen under the banner of Steel, Steam & Stars to raise money for the project. The idea was to hire as many visiting steam engines as possible, draw bigger crowds and reap sizeable dividends; and now the project is well on the way to adding the cylinders, the last major component it needs.

At Llangollen, another major Didcot new-build project is nearing completion, one which will add a major dimension to railway heritage. It is the rebuilding of Great Western railmotor No 93, a vehicle which comprised a steam engine built

Gresley B17 Sandringham 4-6-0 No 2806 Audley End powers through Westerfield near Ipswich. GREAT EASTERN RAILWAY SOCIETY

into a carriage to create a single vehicle, and therefore the forerunner of diesel railcars and diesel and electric multiple units, a concept which forms the mainstay of passenger services in the UK today.

Built in 1908, No 93 was withdrawn as a steam railmotor in 1934. The engine was scrapped but the body was converted to auto coach No 212, and after withdrawal in 1956, survived in Departmental use. The society launched a project to rebuild it to a railmotor in 1998, and in January 2007, an upright boiler manufactured by Israel Newton of Bradford was steamed for the first time. The body of No 92/212, along with a trailer, No 92, are being refurbished at Llangollen, with the aid of substantial Heritage Lottery Fund grant aid, and soon there will be a train set unique in preservation.

Tornado is often described as the first new purpose-designed express passenger steam locomotive (as opposed to mixed traffic engines) to be built in Britain since *Duke of Gloucester* in 1954. Unless you specify gauge, that is not correct, for Didcot is the home of *Firefly*, a replica of the original Daniel Gooch 2-2-2 of 1840 built for Isambard Kingdom Brunel's 7ft 0 ¼in broad gauge Great Western Railway, which was unveiled by the Firefly Trust in 2005 and hauls trains on a demonstration track

– not forgetting, of course, the aforementioned *Iron Duke* replica at the National Railway Museum.

At the Bluebell Railway, a 'semi' new-build project to replicate Brighton Atlantic No 32424 *Beachy Head* is making headway, using a Great Northern Railway Atlantic boiler rediscovered in a woodyard in Essex. The volunteers undertaking the project have claimed that it can be done for around the £300,000 mark, a tenth of the cost of *Tornado*.

Other 'missing gap' projects take an existing locomotive and convert it into another. The Great Western Society has converted GWR 4-6-0 No 4942 *Maindy Hall* into a Saint, the predecessor of the Halls, and it will re-emerge as No 2999 *Lady of Legend*.

A Bluebell Railway group is converting unrestored Barry wreck BR Standard 2MT 2-6-0 No 78059 into the now-extinct 2-6-2 tank engine equivalent as No 84030.

At restored Midsomer Norton station (www.sdjr.co.uk), former Croydon gas works vertical-boilered Sentinel shunter *Joyce* is being transformed into one of two near-identical locomotives which worked for the Somerset & Dorset Joint Railway and then under British Railways, having cut-down cabs to negotiate a low bridge at Radstock.

We now have a line-up of an A1, an A2, an A3 and an A4, and plans are afoot to fill many other holes in the preservation portfolio.

Yet is that all that new-build is about? Certainly not.

For the past 60 years, Britain's heritage railways – now a significant player in the tourist industry – have relied on second-hand locomotives and stock. The purchase of 213 steam engines from Barry scrapyard has made so much possible, but many of its scrap locomotives have taken decades to restore. For example, Bulleid Battle of Britain Pacific No 34059 *Sir Archibald Sinclair* was bought from Barry for the Bluebell Railway in 1979, but did not enter service until April 2009.

Will coming generations be prepared to devote a lifetime of spare hours on a voluntary basis to overhauling the remaining Barry wrecks yet to be tackled, or even maintain and overhaul the ones that have been restored?

The average overhaul of a Barry locomotive has been estimated to cost at least £500,000. Even then, it will still be using historical part-worn parts, and will need some of them to be regularly replaced.

At what point does it become cheaper to build a new locomotive for a heritage line, with the cost being provided by a bank loan serviced by passenger receipts and hire charges?

In theory, a new locomotive should give 20 years or more service on preserved railways without needing a major overhaul, thereby cutting man-hours and costs

And what if a batch of locomotives could be built to supply the needs of several lines?

In 2005, Graham Lee, chairman of rail component provider LH Group Services Ltd, bought what remained of the Hunslet Engine Company of Leeds. He set up new workshops at his private Statfold Barn Railway near Tamworth (www.statfold

barnrailway.co.uk) and began batch-building classic narrow gauge locomotives for sale.

To date, four have been turned out, two 'Quarry Hunslet' 0-4-0 saddle tanks, one with a cab and one without, and two Kerr Stuart 'Wren' class 0-4-0 saddle tanks. More are to follow.

In Germany, Dampflokwerk Meiningen (www.dampflokwerk.de), which built the boiler for *Tornado*, in 2009 went one better – and unveiled an all-new full-size steam locomotive.

No 99.2324, a 900mm gauge 2-8-2T, was built for the 100-mile Bad Doberan-Kuehlungsborn line, which has three similar engines built by Orenstein & Koppel in the 1930s. It began running in at the end of March. Its appearance will no doubt prompt the question – who will be the first to order a new British locomotive from Meiningen and how much would one cost?

The answer may, however, be much closer to home.

At the Severn Valley Railway, the 82045 Locomotive Fund (www.82045.org.uk) is building a new British Railways Standard 3MT 2-6-2 tank engine, an extinct class said to be the perfect-sized locomotive for use on a heritage railway.

And with *Tornado* having been completed, director of engineering David Elliott found himself taking up a fresh challenge, a stone's throw from Darlington Locomotive Works.

In a modern industrial building on the Cleveland Industrial Estate, Darlington's great steam engineering tradition, which includes the A1s, is being kept alive by the Great Northern Steam Company Ltd (www.greatnorthernsteam.co.uk).

As *Tornado* wowed the world with its main line performances, David had his sleeves rolled up again – building an all-new member of another extinct class, the North Eastern Railway's G5 0-4-4 tank engine.

Progress has been rapid, due to the project being funded by five investors who want to run the locomotive on the Weardale Railway in County Durham, a former stomping ground of the type. Thanks to its use of an all-welded boiler and a steel firebox rather than the traditional copper version, the locomotive has been estimated to cost in the region of £400,000 – and a second one could easily be built using the same patterns.

Great Northern has had two decades of building steam, beginning with model and miniature locomotives and traction engines and building up to full-size ones.

The firm supplied two full-size replicas of the unusual diminutive *Ant* and *Bee* 0-4-0s for the reborn 19in gauge Great Laxey Mines Railway on the Isle of Man. Now having amassed a wealth of experience and expertise, the firm is capable of much bigger projects – and is planning to move into bigger premises to build a North Eastern Railway V class 4-4-2 in time for the 2012 Olympic Games.

Can the firm do it? Well, it now has a track record, and also *Tornado's* director of engineering on board. Furthermore, in terms of main line running, the A1 Trust, in overcoming so many hurdles, has blazed the trail for others to follow.

BE PART OF THE
SUCCESS STORY...

Help keep *Tornado* on the main line

Back in 1990, a few people had a dream. Since then thousands of people have come together to make that dream a reality. The result is Britain's first purpose-built standard gauge express passenger Pacific steam locomotive since No 71000 *Duke of Gloucester* in 1954, and the first Pacific since Britannias Nos 70053 *Moray Firth* and 70054 *Dornoch Firth* in September the same year.

Since it was finished, the new Peppercorn A1 has proved a big draw wherever it's been, whether hauling the Royal Train or the prestigious Venice-Simplon Orient Express Pullman, visiting the National Railway Museum or heritage railways or pulling the first through steam train between London and Edinburgh in over 40 years for the BBC.

So *Tornado* is finished, but we can't afford to be complacent. The huge costs of building a new main line steam locomotive for the 21st century mean that the A1 still owes hundreds of thousands of pounds – £700,000 at the time of writing – and these debts must be paid off to ensure that she has a secure working main line future.

For that reason, we do hope you'll be able to support us generously. There are many ways you can do so, starting from a monthly covenant (from just £5). Some of the ways you can help Tornado are detailed below – or feel free to drop us a line through one of the ways listed and our team will be happy to explain more.

The last of the renowned Peppercorn class A1 steam locomotives was, tragically, scrapped in 1966. But a brand new £3-million A1, No 60163 *Tornado*, has been brought to life – and we urgently need your help to keep it on the main line.

The Peppercorn A1s were the last of the great express passenger locomotives designed by the London & North Eastern Railway. British Railways built 49 of them at its Doncaster and Darlington works in 1948/9. Throughout the 1950s the majestic A1s pulled luxury Pullman trains from London to Yorkshire and the North East.

They were the last word in speed, style and glamour – but none escaped the scrapman's torch.

The A1 Steam Locomotive Trust – a registered charity – has built a completely new A1 to the original design and with the help of the latest technology. Fitted with additional water capacity and the latest railway safety electronics, *Tornado* is fully equipped for today's main line railway.

We already have hundreds of supporters and the backing of the best of British business – including William Cook Cast Products, National Express East Coast, Rolls-Royce, Corus and BAe Systems – helping to raise the £700,000 needed to keep Tornado on the main line.

Tornado is now complete and operating on Network Rail. However, for this to continue we still need your help – and you too can come on board for the price of a pint!

That was our concept when we launched the project in 1990. Supporters could covenant (donate) just the monthly equivalent of the price of a pint of beer per week. Beer cost £1.25 a pint in the North East then – today it is over £2.50!

Much of the locomotive as you see it today has been funded by this means – a large number of people contributing a small amount on a regular basis. Although Deeds of Covenant have now been replaced by Gift Aid, the trust is still able to claim back from the Inland Revenue the income/capital gains tax that you have paid on your donations.

For every £10 that you donate, the trust could claim an additional £2.82, making your contribution worth £12.82.

By becoming a regular donor you can play your part in making history – it's that simple. We hope you're able to help us to keep *Tornado* on the main line.

Simply fill in the attached form – photocopy it if you do not wish to cut the page.

Model maker Bachmann has had a Peppercorn A1 in its range for several years. A special limited edition in BR Brunswick green was produced for A1 Trust covenators, who in 2008 had the chance to buy one in the works grey livery that it carried while undergoing its test runs. Bachmann has now updated the model and reissued it as No 60163 Tornado, taking on board all the modifications to the original design where appropriate. Like the real thing, it has been issued in British Railways apple green livery. BACHMANN

HOW YOU CAN DONATE

Please join us and help keep Tornado on the main line through one of our several types of donation:

Regular donations
A monthly payment made by standing order in units of £5. In recognition of your support, you will receive:

- A print of the last Peppercorn class A1 60145 Saint Mungo by Dougal Cameron
- Access to view Tornado at all reasonable times
- The Trust's journal and newsletters on a regular basis
- The opportunity to attend the trust's annual convention
- The opportunity to attend days out at other railway centres
- Priority travel on Trust-organised trains hauled by Tornado
- Your name inscribed on the Roll of Honour at Darlington Locomotive Works

Dedicated donations
You may wish to support the project by linking your donation to a specific part already on the locomotive.

Dedicated donations can be used to remember a loved one, celebrate a birthday or any other occasion. The part of the certificate that recognises the individual – and occasion – to whom the donation is dedicated can be produced with the wording of your choice.

To recognise your support, dedicated donors have:

- The name inscribed on the Roll of Honour at Darlington Locomotive Works, which will detail the parts sponsored
- A certificate recording the details of the sponsorship and a copy of the engineering drawing for the part sponsored

For a list of parts available and their cost please telephone our hotline 01325 4 60163 or email to dcovs@a1steam.com

Bond Issue
In order to be able to fund the boiler for Tornado, the Trust launched a £500,000 bond issue. The bond issue has raised more than £400,000 to date, is still open, pays four per cent and is repayable between December 2012 and December 2016. For a full prospectus please telephone our hotline 01325 4 60163 or email to enquiries@a1steam.com

Single donations
Single donations for any amount are most welcome at any time.

Yes! I would like to help keep Tornado on the main line

Please complete the form below and return to:

The A1 Steam Locomotive Trust
FREEPOST DL861
Darlington Locomotive Works
Hopetown Lane
Darlington DL3 6RQ

No stamp is required. We will then send you the appropriate forms for your standing order and, where applicable, a Gift Aid form so that we can reclaim UK income tax paid.

For further information on any aspect of supporting the Trust please:
Call our 'hotline' on: 01325 4 60163
Visit our website at: www.a1steam.com
Email to: enquiries@a1steam.com

Amount you would like to donate:

£ _____ per month

£ _____ single donation

PLEASE WRITE IN BLOCK CAPITALS
Name _____
Address _____
_____ Postcode _____
Email _____
Telephone _____
Signature _____
Date _____

I am a UK taxpayer and would like you to treat this donation as a Gift Aid Donation. You must pay an amount of income tax and/or Capital Gains Tax at least equal to the tax that the trust reclaims on your donations in this tax year (currently 28p for every £1 you give). ☐

Thank you for your valued support – together we can keep Tornado on the main line!